IMAGES
of America

FORT VALLEY

This image shows Fort Valley in its heyday. Every storefront is occupied and open for business five days a week from 9:00 a.m. to 6:00 p.m. and later on Saturday. Three major routes (Georgia 49, Georgia 96, and US 341) crisscross downtown, as seen here around 1948, and intersect again at Five Points. It was two-way traffic on these streets. The Holly Tree pinpoints Fincher Park, more commonly known as the Triangle. The panel truck and Odorless Cleaners are owned by Wallis Hardeman, and the café on the right is Poole's Café, where the coffee drinkers would meet and exchange news daily. It was owned and operated by "Dud" and Mae Poole and was known for its barbecue and Brunswick stew. In the 1960s, new owner Joe Mullis renamed it Mullis Café. With the completion of US Interstate 75 (roughly 10 miles east) in the 1970s, downtown Fort Valley instantaneously lost a significant portion of its automobile traffic and business trade. (Courtesy of the *Leader-Tribune*.)

On the Cover: The Fort Valley High School Green Waves Marching Band is pictured in 1947 marching down Main Street. It was the first year for the newly formed band under the direction of Leon Culpepper, and the first football team was coached by Ned Warren. With every downtown storefront occupied, it is clear that Fort Valley is doing well. Shopping, dining, and entertainment are all here as seen in the variety of stores on the left: Avera's (Rexall Drug), Johnson's Clothing, Old Exchange Bank, Khoury's Department Store, Carither's Furniture Store (Norge Appliances sign), Fashion Shoppe, Harrison Brothers Grocery (Coca-Cola sign), the *Leader-Tribune* newspaper, and unidentified (Westinghouse Appliances). On the right, part of the Peach Theatre (also known as the Austin Theatre) marquee is visible as well as the Liberty Café (also known as Chris's Café), and the Winona Hotel. (Courtesy of Nick Strickland.)

IMAGES
of America

FORT VALLEY

Gilda E. Stanbery and James E. Khoury

ARCADIA
PUBLISHING

ISBN 978-0-7385-9089-9

Published by Arcadia Publishing
Charleston, South Carolina

Printed in the United States of America

Library of Congress Control Number: 2012944676

For all general information, please contact Arcadia Publishing:
Telephone 843-853-2070
Fax 843-853-0044
E-mail sales@arcadiapublishing.com
For customer service and orders:
Toll-Free 1-888-313-2665

Visit us on the Internet at www.arcadiapublishing.com

This work is dedicated to the endurance of Fort Valley and its people—past, present, and future. And to our families and friends—without their patience, love, and support, this project would not have been possible.

CONTENTS

ACKNOWLEDGMENTS

This book is prepared with the support of Peach Public Libraries Local History Collection and with the permission of the Peach Public Libraries Board of Trustees. Several library staff assisted in a variety of ways, in particular Jane Matthews and Billy Tripp.

The contents of these pages reveal a glimpse of Fort Valley's history by exposing the reader to images from the past. Information presented here provides only a framework for a more complete history of the people and places that make Fort Valley unique.

Preparation of this book has truly been an enlightening, sometimes challenging, and enjoyable experience. Seeing the pages of history unfold has been rewarding and has engendered unparalleled respect and admiration for the men and women who have worked untiringly to sustain Fort Valley through the years.

It is a great risk that we could overlook the inclusion of someone among the following who have contributed to this work, for which we are most appreciative: the *Leader-Tribune*, the Peach County Historical Society, Jim Teabow, T.J. Crutchfield, Marilyn Neisler Windham, Kay Hardeman Meyer, Wallis Hardeman, Nick Strickland, Frank Dean Martin III, Wilmetta Langston, Helen Rhea Luce Stumbo, Latrelle Giles Alford, Ann Blair Brown, Claire Houser-Dodd, W.C. Wyatt, Wilton Walton, Peggy and Dennis Herbert, Debbie Spearman, Delise and Paul Knight, W.L. Brown, Rich Bennett, Jann Culpepper, Debbie Dunning Liipfert, Frank Duke, Marion Allen, Todd Bryan, Elizabeth Harris White, Jimmy Smith, Dorothy Myers Crumbly, Albert O'Bryant, Troy Whatley, Barbara and Billy Davidson, Dr. David Marshall, William "Bill" Marshall, Riley Kinney, Jo Wilson, Bonnie and Kent Wirsing, Gay Gillespie Faircloth, Matt Mullis, Jeff Doles, Walter Haussner, Betty Cleveland, Barbara Ray, Jamie Sanders Arnold, Carole Hutto Odom, Gary Sheffield, Betty Parham McGee, Clifford Ponder, June Preston See, Vision Bear, Jan and Tim McCord, Fort Valley State University Archives, Mary Jean and Ken Banter, Danny Gilleland, Eileen Lovett Weber, Clayton Luce, Duke Lane Jr., Sandra Ethleen Howell Davis, Steve Nowicki, Sarah Hall Eliassen, Natalie Khoury Ridgewell, and Andrea Khoury. A very special thanks to Cheryl Gill Khoury and to Taylor L.C. for her many contributions, from computer rescue to drawing maps to frappe delivery.

Our history is in our people. The one lasting impression from our work is the urgent need to record and preserve our history. The images in this volume appear courtesy of the Peach Public Libraries Local History Collection in the Thomas Public Library and the authors, James E. Khoury and Gilda E. Stanbery, unless otherwise noted.

INTRODUCTION

The first Fort Valley residents were Creeks from the Muskogee and Euchee tribes. Some of the first European explorers to come to America made their way up the Flint River and found a society of people who had inhabited the land for thousands of years, cutting paths through the forests, canoeing the rivers, and planting the fields. Those trails served the needs of native populations by connecting their villages with one another and allowing them to travel great distances in quest of game, fish, shellfish, and pearls, as well as such mineral resources as salt, flint, pipestone, steatite, hematite, and ochre.

Gen. James Oglethorpe used the system of trails to lay out his new colony in 1733, providing settlers with sites to establish trading posts and to intercept trade from the natives. George Washington sent Benjamin Hawkins to serve as Indian agent when the clash of the two cultures seemed imminent, but Hawkins could not ward off the inevitable. This part of the country was necessary to the manifest destiny of Thomas Jefferson and was the proving ground for the fierce nationalism of Andrew Jackson. The Indian Removal Act delivered the final blow to the Southeast's natives by brutally and methodically removing one nation to assure the survival of another—thus securing Georgia lands for white settlement. As one of the largest slave-holding regions in the antebellum South, where cotton was king, it would later foster the civil rights movement.

Between 1820 and the start of the Civil War in 1861, numerous counties were carved out of the land between the Flint and Ocmulgee Rivers. Settlements sprang up along riverbanks or where major paths converged as the first traders began to enter Creek Territory. James Abbington Everett, Fort Valley's founding father, first married Cussenna Barnard, daughter of Timpoochie Barnard, a Creek leader and signer of the 1821 Treaty of Indian Springs. This ensured Everett's welcome among the Creeks and granted him ownership of a large land reserve at the signing of the treaty. Fort Valley Post Office, Crawford County, Georgia, was established on December 7, 1825. Applicants Everett and Mathew Dorsey named it after Arthur Fort, a Revolutionary War hero, legislator, politician, and land speculator. Everett was the postmaster until 1834. Initially located at Everett's Crawford County home, the post office was moved to his new house in Houston County and later to Everett's trading post in present downtown Fort Valley. Fort Valley initially grew up around the post office. Other first settlers were Peter Greene and William and Allen Wiggins. Everett contributed greatly to the development of Fort Valley and other areas of Georgia. He donated land and money toward the construction of a church and school on Everett Square. He purchased railroad stock, as did others, to persuade the Southwestern Railroad Company to run through town. The first train arrived in 1852.

The town had 250 people, three stores, one academy, and one church in 1849. The first school, Fort Valley Manual Training School, was established in 1828. Fort Valley Academy, established by legislative act and sustained by tuition, was chartered in 1836. Grady Institute (1886) was the first public school. Dr. Ralph Newton was the first superintendent of Fort Valley Schools, the first president of Kiwanis, a Peach Blossom Festival chairman, and chairman of the Thomas Public

Library Board. While not the first school superintendent, Ernest R. Anderson has certainly been the longest serving, from 1945 to 1984.

The Old Pond Church (1840) was the first church in Fort Valley and was later renamed Fort Valley United Methodist Church. Usher's Temple Church was established in 1866 as the first free African American church. Isaac Anderson, who helped build Usher's Temple Church, also began the "Colored Methodist Church" in the South in 1870. As a result, Usher's Temple nurtured the growth of St. Peter's A.M.E. and Shiloh Baptist, both on Griffin Lane, and Fort Valley High and Industrial School (1895) resulted from their planning conferences. Houston County Negro Extension agent Otis O'Neal held the first Ham Show in 1916; later, after Margaret L. Toomer joined, it became the famous Ham and Egg Show. Fort Valley High and Industrial School became Fort Valley Normal and Industrial School with a junior college rating in 1929. Henry A. Hunt succeeded John Davison in 1919 as head of the school, which was now affiliated with the Episcopal Church. The history of Fort Valley State University had been put in motion.

Fort Valley was chartered by a legislative act approved on March 3, 1856, with Charles D. Anderson, William H. Hollinshead, William I. Greene, Adolphus D. Kendrick, and Dr. David N. Austin appointed as commissioners. They were empowered by the legislature to "make laws and regulations for a government in the best interest of the citizens" and were appointed to serve until their successors were elected. Dr. William Mathews, state representative for Houston County, in which Fort Valley was then located, introduced the bill for incorporation. When Fort Valley was incorporated, it was the largest city in Houston County. Lafayette Cherry published the earliest known newspaper, the *19th Century*, in 1858.

The Fort Valley Fire Department (FVFD) started in August 1893, and A.S. Martin was the first fire chief. Martin came to Fort Valley to run a foundry and built a grand home on Persons Street. FVFD used a horse-drawn fire wagon before the first motorized fire truck was put into service in 1915. The first African American firefighter, Joe Walker, joined the department in 1943.

The original charter established the town limits as one mile in each direction from the railroad depot. Outside the one-mile radius, large plantations grew up, devoted at first to cotton and later to peaches, apples, wheat, asparagus, and pecans. The development of Samuel Rumph's Elberta and Eugene Hiley's Georgia Belle and Hiley Belle peach varieties, hydro-cooling, refrigerated railcars, and excellent rail connections carrying fresh fruit great distances combined to make Fort Valley the peach-growing center of Georgia. For the next 50 years, peach was king.

In the four years of the Civil War (1861–1865), the South was the primary battleground, with all but two of the major battles taking place on Southern soil. To the north of Fort Valley is Macon, an important quartermaster center for the Confederacy that distributed supplies, ordnance, and munitions to armies in the field. The fighting in Atlanta and surrounding areas made Fort Valley, Macon, and other communities important hospital and refugee centers, swelling their populations. Fort Valley had an 1864 Buckner and Gamble hospital of record, as well as several temporary hospitals in what are now Fort Valley's historic homes and structures. In the city's Oaklawn Cemetery, a historical marker stands where more than 20 unknown Confederate soldiers are buried, reading "Patriotic men and women of this vicinity assisted in the care of the sick and wounded." A memorial to honor all veterans was erected at Everett Square in 2008.

A catastrophic fire destroyed nearly all the downtown buildings on October 31, 1867. Business was discouraged by a major bank robbery of $12,000 on March 4, 1872, and a financial panic further depressed the area. By 1881, the town had replaced the wooden buildings with brick, enticed a second railroad to Fort Valley, and was prospering from the new peach industry. These years were among the city's best.

No record of the first elected officials has been found. In 1882, Judge A.C. Riley Sr. of Perry bought a home on College Street, and he lived there until his death. Voted into office on April 9, 1888, he is the first-known elected mayor. Riley resigned on January 7, 1890, and Joseph Lafayette Fincher, a jeweler by profession, served until the next election in April 1890. It was not until 1953 that a city hall was constructed and the city records and offices had a permanent home. Prior to that, the city was administered from the water and light plant located near the Harris House

Hotel, later the Winona Hotel. The youngest mayor, Marion Allen, had to wait until his 25th birthday to take office on December 28, 1954. In 1962, Ann Frances Mitchell Vinson became the first and, to date, only woman to hold the office of mayor of Fort Valley, Georgia. She was also known for her chauffeur-driven Rolls-Royce and her husband, Dr. Frank Vinson, who had his medical practice in Fort Valley.

Downtown Fort Valley grew up between the post office and the west side of the rail line. It began with the trading post, livery, and tavern. The trails became roads, there were more settlers, and the stagecoach and post office arrived. More settlers meant more merchants, and the town grew. The area's future, as well as that of the rest of the state, lay with railroads after the Civil War. Fort Valley benefited and prospered from having both freight and passenger rail services. By 1911, Fort Valley had a population of 3,000 people and offered convenient service for rail travelers in the presence of hotels, boardinghouses, and restaurants. Cotton still passed through Fort Valley, but the peach industry had become the leading money crop in Middle Georgia by the turn of the 20th century. It was the railroad that helped make the town in general, and the vast peach orchards in particular, an economic success from 1900 to 1927. The 1920s marked the peak of railroad operations. The trains no longer stop in Fort Valley for passengers.

One-third of Georgia's peaches were grown around Fort Valley, known as the "Peach Paradise." The idea to celebrate the peach resulted in Fort Valley's five Peach Blossom Festivals from 1922 to 1926. Each year, when the peach trees were a sea of pink blossoms, tens of thousands would come for the parades, pageants, and barbecue. The peach brought attention and prosperity not only to Fort Valley but also to the state of Georgia. When Peach County was officially created in 1924, it made sense to name it after the peach and to name Fort Valley as the county seat. The 1930 census indicates Fort Valley's population had increased 50 percent to 4,560 people in a brief 20-year period.

As Fort Valley grew, the need for merchants, banks, doctors, lawyers, and others with specific skills and talents increased. In addition to the peach industry, other industry had gained a foothold: Woolfolk Chemical Works, Anthoine Machine Shop, Pearson Basket Mill, Happyvale Flour Mill, Wright and Solomon, Inc. (Jolly Nut Company), and Atlantic Ice Company (the world's largest ice plant) to name a few. Blue Bird Body Company, established in 1927, would quickly become a major employer and an international company known for its high-quality school buses with global operations. Fort Valley State College's steady growth, increasing campus, and enrollment earned it university status.

Fort Valley's importance in an agricultural region rich in cotton and peaches as the central interchange between field and where multiple roads converged to bring produce to the rail diminished as the importance of highway transportation increased. The most significant change came with the installation of I-75. Before that, one of the nation's longest interstate highway systems, the Dixie Highway Association—from Sault Sainte Marie, Michigan, to Miami, Florida—came through Fort Valley. It remained the crossroads for several Georgia highways, and with the Dixie Highway development, commercial activities began to expand. At their height in the 1960s, there were over 30 full-service gas stations and three truck stops in Fort Valley for the tourist and commercial trade. Fort Valley was home to large hotels and boardinghouses for travelers and those associated with seasonal work due to the railroad and agriculture. In 1926, US 341 was commissioned. At the same time, the Dixie Highway was renumbered as Georgia 49, and the Dixie Highway's north-south traffic shifted to US 19 and US 41. Touring motorists in the mid-20th century traveled through Fort Valley to and from the historic Andersonville prison camp via the Dixie Highway, or what some call the Andersonville Trail. If traveling east-west through town, one does so either on the Presidential Parkway (Georgia 96) or the Golden Isles Parkway (US 341).

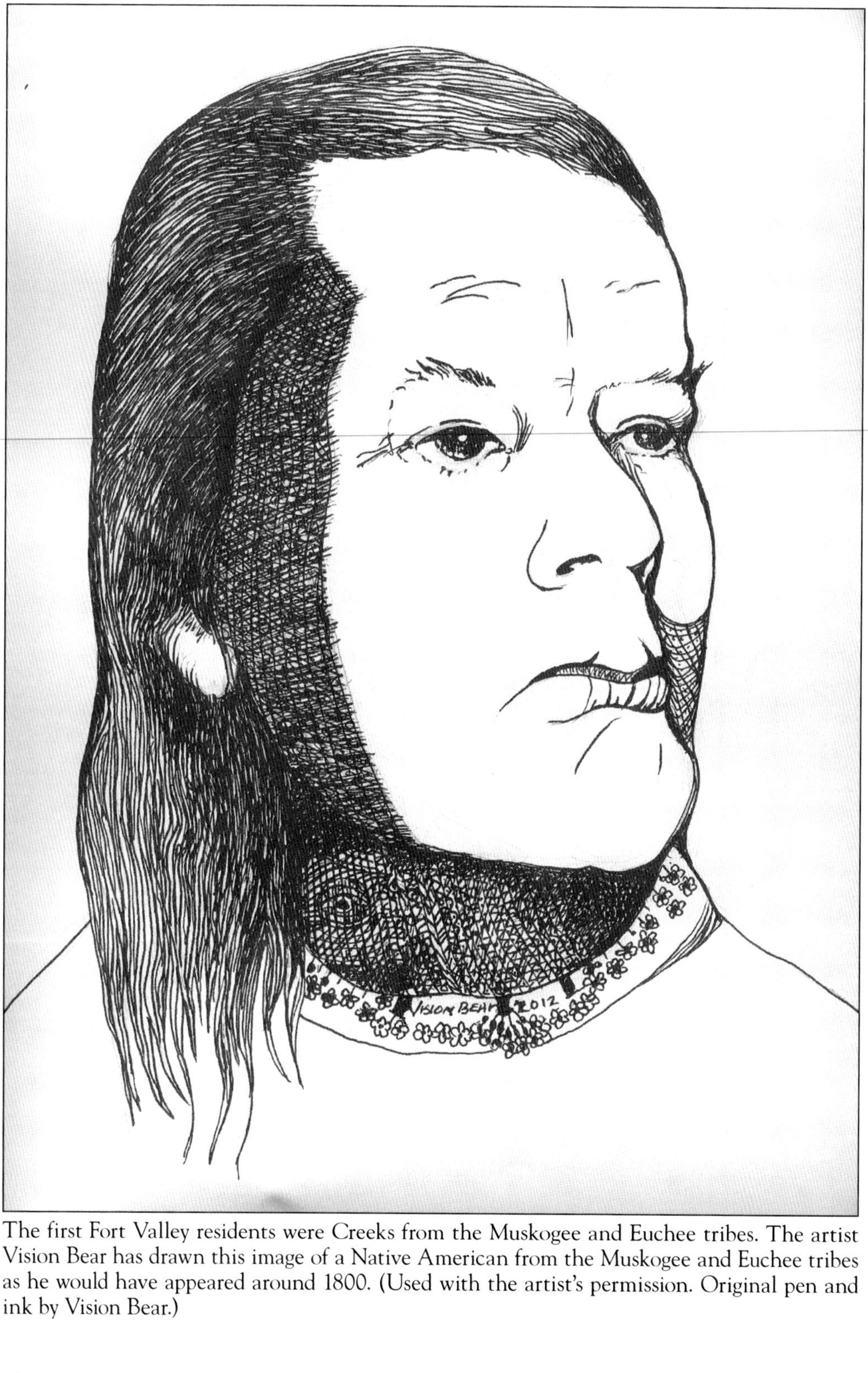

The first Fort Valley residents were Creeks from the Muskogee and Euchee tribes. The artist Vision Bear has drawn this image of a Native American from the Muskogee and Euchee tribes as he would have appeared around 1800. (Used with the artist's permission. Original pen and ink by Vision Bear.)

One

Historic Homes

The majority of Fort Valley's neighborhoods were built during two peaks of great prosperity that parallel the growth of the railroad—the 1880s and again in the 1920s—and which were part of Fort Valley's heyday as a transportation, agricultural, and political hub in the newly formed Peach County.

The first of the two periods of significant growth is reflected stylistically with Victorian examples built in the 19th century by the most affluent along West Church Street and Anderson Avenue. Everett Square, named a National Register Historic District in 1994, contains an excellent collection of homes constructed in the late 1860s that reflects the lifestyles of middle- to upper-middle class working families. The next growth period was pre–World War I through 1930, when many Georgian Revival–style houses were built south of Central Avenue. Older homes were replaced by the early-20th-century elite in the Everett Square district with custom designs by prominent local architects.

Historic homes are often the most modest homes outside of a historic district. Their importance and significance should not be overlooked. Full city blocks of Craftsman bungalows and minimal traditional cottages came with the expanding working and middle class in the early to mid-20th century along Knoxville, Persons, Riley, Vineville, North Miller, and other streets surrounding a new high school. Clean, refined houses of the post–World War II era sit between early 20th-century bungalows and gable-end Depression-era Georgian cottages along North Miller Street.

The residential historic district also contains public buildings and churches, and many are described in the chapter "Historic Structures." Fort Valley's oldest cemetery, Oaklawn, has an abundance of historical markers where several founding family members are buried, and there is a Confederate memorial site.

Those historical homes identified within are only a small representation of the hidden treasures to be found in Fort Valley.

The c. 1870 Troutman House is of the Greek Revival style and is one of the large stately homes built around Fort Valley. Standing at the end of Main Street, it has a dramatic and grand appearance. Col. John Fielding Troutman Sr., the original owner, was a state senator and served on the staff of Gov. Howell Cobb. The house originally sat several thousand yards southeast of its present location in a grove of trees surrounded by pastureland. Between 1906 and 1920, after Troutman Sr. died, John F. Troutman Jr. had the house moved to where it is today. The Peach Blossom Festivals from 1922 to 1926 were held on the property, and as many as 50,000 people attended annually. The house has been repurposed as offices for the Peach County Chamber of Commerce, Peach County Development Authority, Fort Valley Main Street, and the Georgia Peach Festival.

This West Church Street Colonial Revival–style house, built around 1912, highlights its Ionic columns with a center portico spanning two stories. It stands next to the Peach County Courthouse, across the street from Fort Valley City Hall, Fire Department, and Police Department. It is pictured here as Rooks Funeral Home, owned by Stafford Rooks, who was also the county coroner. The funeral home moved to the other side of the courthouse, and the family business continues with son Kerry Rooks, who also became coroner. The house is now Village Realty, owned and operated by real estate broker and Fort Valley City Council member Elizabeth "Beth" Mathews Collins.

W.C. Wright, a local druggist and peach farmer, built this home in 1922 on West Church Street at a cost of $125,000. Wright unfortunately died two weeks before his family was to move in. In 1958, the local woman's club purchased the property for its headquarters. It has since returned to its former life as a private residence, with Wright's great-grandson Frank Freshwater and his family living there. The house is in the Italian Renaissance style with a low-pitched roof covered by Ludowici–Celedon "Imperial" shale roofing tiles.

On the corner of Miller Street and Central Avenue, this Colonial Revival–style house is similar to the house on Church Street in that it highlights its Ionic columns with a center portico spanning two stories. Benjamin Thomas Marshall built the house around 1913 on what was part of the site for the Grady Institute, the first public school. He was a local wholesale grocer and active in the Methodist Church. (Courtesy of Helen Rhea Luce Stumbo.)

Albert J. Evans built this predominately Italian Renaissance Revival–style house in 1916 on the site of the first public school, the Grady Institute. The eclectic architectural style features Colonial Revival–influenced porches and Craftsman–influenced eaves and windows. The house is also known for the use of Classical detailing throughout. Evans was known as the "Peach King." As a peach broker in the 1920s, he controlled the price of peaches on the Eastern Seaboard. Although he lost his fortune in the Great Depression, he successfully rebuilt his business. Evans also served more than 40 years as a member of the board of education. He was a Fort Valley High and Industrial School trustee as well as a trustee for Atlanta Trust Company and Mercer University. (Courtesy of Helen Rhea Luce Stumbo.)

Samuel Rumph, credited as a founder of the Georgia peach industry, built this College Street house for his mother, Caroline, in 1894. This house has features from several different styles of the Victorian period. The end and front cross gables were used in many Queen Anne houses. The shingles, curved windows of the gables, and dormers were frequently used in shingle-style houses. (Courtesy of Marilyn Neisler Windham.)

Built in the 1850s on College Street, this house was part of the Fort Valley Female Seminary, chartered in 1852. During the Civil War, it was used as a Confederate hospital, and the Georgia Blind Asylum occupied the house. After the war, the asylum moved to Macon and became the Academy for the Blind. In 1880, the Fort Valley Academy moved into the house with 24 boys and girls and a live-in headmaster, Prof. Thomas B. Russell. John W. Woolfolk bought the house in 1912, renovated it, and added porches and the brick veneer. The corner brick quoins were commonly found on Italianate-style and Italian Renaissance Revival–style houses. Woolfolk, a deacon in the Presbyterian Church, purchased the Thomas Chemical Company plant in 1923.

Henry Clickett Harris built this three-story home around 1880 on the northwest corner of College Street and Everett Square. The three gables with two bay windows and the parapet (similar to the one on his hotel) were unique. Unfortunately, the grand house with its crystal chandeliers, wrought ironwork, and lookout burned. Harris's construction company had built many of the brick buildings downtown to replace the wooden ones destroyed in the 1867 fire. In 1881, he built the Harris House Hotel, later known as the Winona Hotel, on Main Street facing the railroad tracks.

One of Fort Valley's oldest, this Everett Square home was built by Peter Greene prior to 1850. His daughter, Mary Beaufort Greene, married his close friend and Fort Valley's founding father, James Abingdon Everett. Grady Institute professor W.J. Scroggs and family lived here at one time as well. Descendants of Joseph E. Davidson, Peach County's first state representative, have occupied the home since 1930. The single-story porch has been "Victorianized."

Originally, this West Church Street home, built in 1912, was occupied by J.D. Wilson, a wholesale and retail grocer. It was later sold to Felton Hatcher in 1937. One of the doorways in the main hall was used to track the growth of the three Hatcher daughters—reminders of its history. Hatcher was a Texaco distributor and farmer. He served on the Fort Valley City Council, Fort Valley School Board, Fort Valley Draft Board, Thomas Public Library Board, Peach County Hospital Authority, Pines Needles Country Club Board, and the vestry of St. Andrew's Episcopal Church. (Courtesy of Helen Rhea Luce Stumbo.)

This Knoxville Street house was built around 1880 by George P. Greene, a local druggist who had a grocery and hardware store on Main Street. It has an *L*-shaped plan with end gables and a cross gable, popular in the Victorian era. The decorative spindle work on both the upper and lower floors of the porch is unusual. Greene paid $250 for this land in 1875. The house was originally a cottage before being enlarged to two stories, and a bedroom addition was done before 1940.

This postcard shows a "Bird's-Eye View of Fort Valley, GA, Looking North" around 1908. Take notice of the heavy canopy of trees protecting the homes and streets from the sun and summer heat. There is limited evidence of automobiles; it appears horses still dominate the dirt streets.

Based on the position of the water tower in the background, this photograph was taken between 1926 and 1931. The gas station and café to the left is the future site of the post office built in 1932. The house across the street survives today as Village Realty. In 1936, the Peach County Courthouse was constructed next to it. To the right of the grassy area in the foreground is the future site of Fort Valley City Hall, which was constructed in 1953, giving the city records and offices a permanent home.

The Persons Street neighborhood, as seen here looking west from Macon Street around 1916, has a diverse stock of residential forms and significant architectural styles. With the expanding working and middle classes in the early 20th century came the construction of Craftsman bungalows and minimal traditional cottages. Persons Street is named in honor of one of Fort Valley's founding families. Rev. George Washington Persons was one of eight men who paid the debt of Georgia Female Academy, now Wesleyan College. His two-story brick home stood at the head of Persons and Knoxville Streets. It is noted for its reverse staircase, built so that the young men waiting in the hall could not get a glimpse of his daughter's ankles.

The Anderson Avenue neighborhood, also named in honor of early Fort Valleyans, reflects the more affluent Victorian-style homes of the 19th century. The nearer the house is to Church Street, the more likely it is to be grander in size and style. Charles D. Anderson was one of the original commissioners when Fort Valley was incorporated in 1856. William J. Anderson had his home and plantation at the end of Anderson Avenue. He is considered one of Fort Valley's early merchants and businessmen, as he established the first bank in town, Planter's Bank.

Built in the 1860s by Stephen Elisha Bassett facing the tracks on Commercial Heights, this town house reflects the importance of the relationship between the railroads and the farmer seeing his crops off to market. The gains in rail shipping productivity did not necessarily translate into lower rates for farmers and thus higher farm gate prices, and the real rates were highly variable between 1865 and 1900. Bassett also built Pineola Plantation and the Congregational (Methodist) Church on Persons Street and was one of the founders of Fort Valley State College (FVSC). (Courtesy of Marilyn Neisler Windham.)

The Anderson House (also known as the Honor House), the oldest facility on the Fort Valley State University campus, was the residence of Francis W. Gano. Gano came from Michigan, purchased a large tract of land from Capt. John F. Houser, then divided it into lots and sold it to African Americans. He was one of the founders of Fort Valley High and Industrial School (FVHIS). The house was renovated in 1918 and served as the family homes for FVHIS principal Henry A. Hunt, FVSC president Horace Mann Bond, and FVSC president Cornelius V. Troup. It was named in memory of Benjamin S. Anderson, who served as professor of agriculture during FVSC's early years.

James A. Everett, the founding father of Fort Valley, built this home about 1834. It originally sat near the Old Atlanta Highway north of Fort Valley. At some point, it became a retail establishment known as Jeanes Antiques. It was moved to its present site on Northwoods Drive in 1982. This two-story plantation plain–type home was renovated and its historic integrity was preserved by Jann and Bryant Culpepper. Built out of heart pine, the home originally had one large room on the top floor and two below with six fireplaces throughout. It is in the National Register of Historic Places. It is the oldest house in Fort Valley and in Peach County. (Both, courtesy of Jann and Bryant Culpepper.)

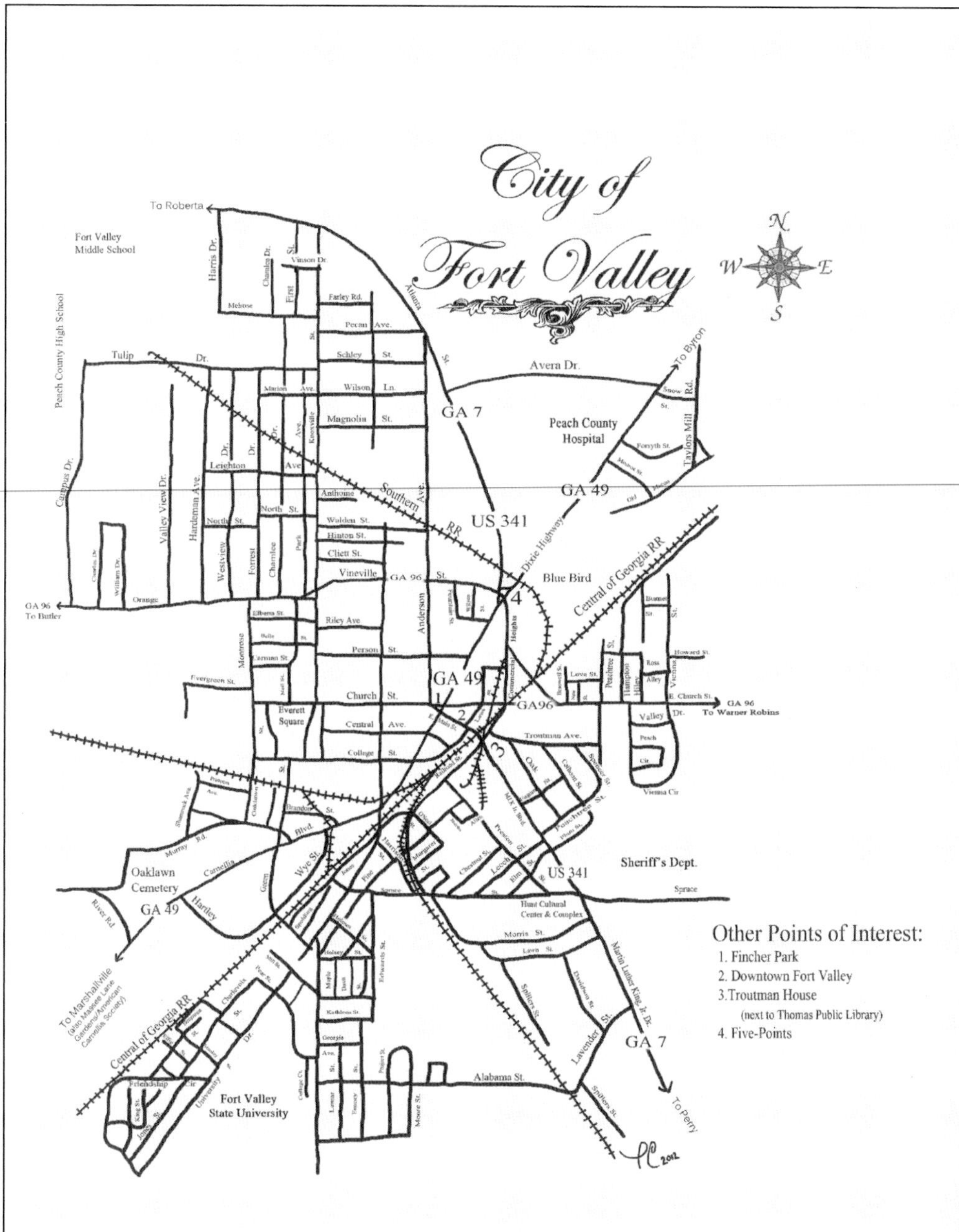

Shown here is a map of Fort Valley featuring the intersection of major railroad lines and highways that influenced the history of the city. (Used with the artist's permission. Original by Taylor L.C.)

Two

Historic Structures

Most of the images in this chapter represent the special attributes of both commercial and residential areas that define the character of Fort Valley's historic structures. Many of these buildings are well over 100 years old, and a number of businesses have operated from them. Where possible, a look inside these structures and the businesses that were there is included.

The Railroad and Industrial District is Fort Valley's apex. Three rail lines merge downtown, where passenger and freight depots, a switching tower, and ancillary industry are located. There are several large brick shed-style buildings in the area. It includes properties along North and South Camellia Boulevard from just south of Five Points, both sides of the railroad, and the properties along Commercial Heights.

The Commercial District originates at the oldest buildings along Lowe Street (formerly Railroad Street) facing the tracks; Main and Church Streets form a core triangle on the east side of Camellia Boulevard. On the west side of Camellia Boulevard, another triangle is formed with Main and Church Streets. The center of that triangle is named Fincher Park for Joseph Lafayette Fincher, a jeweler on Main Street. He was Fort Valley's mayor for three full terms (1904–1910) and a steward in the Methodist Church. Fincher Park is the site of Everett's Trading Post, Fort Valley's first storage water tank, the Holly Tree, and more recently a gazebo and the chiming town clock donated by Dr. Daniel and Muriel (Halprin) Nathan. Camellia Boulevard (also called Georgia 49, Dixie Highway, and Macon Street) contributed to the downtown shifting from a rail center to a highway crossroad.

The Fort Valley State University (FVSU) campus has an abundance of historic structures surrounding the quadrangle, where several founding members are buried. FVSU is an 1890s land grant institution, and its origins are entwined with Fort Valley High and Industrial School (1895). Many of these early buildings bear the names of individuals or churches that funded their construction.

Due to limitations, several historic structures could not be featured, such as Massee Lane Gardens, Pineola Plantation's home and cotton barn, the J.D. Fagan Farmhouse, the Old Jail House, the Woolfolk Building, the Austin Theatre, the Atlantic Ice Company, and several churches. The historical structures identified within are only a small representation of Fort Valley's hidden treasures.

Here is an early look at downtown Fort Valley. Originally wooden structures, after the 1867 fire nearly destroyed all of Main Street, they were replaced with brick buildings. Shops were located on the street level, and living quarters or professional office spaces were above.

This 50,000-gallon water tower would be removed from Fincher Park in 1925 and replaced with a self-cleaning 200,000-gallon tower behind the city utilities to accommodate the growing city's needs. In the 1926 Peach Blossom Festival photographs taken in the Fincher Park area, where Church and Main Streets intersect, there is no trace of the tower.

This is a view of Railroad Street looking north. The three-story building on the left is the New Dixie Hotel, and at the end of the street is the early Coca-Cola Bottling Company. This postcard is a good look at how the architecture and the downtown environment were influenced by the use of horse and wagon as everyday transportation.

By 1914, the streetscape was electrified, city water and fire hydrants were installed, and sidewalks were paved. The dirt streets were surfaced with cinders from the coal the city used to provide electricity. City officials oversee the installation of utilities. (Courtesy of Marilyn Neisler Windham.)

Looking west around 1900, these buildings face Church Street (also called Colored Street and Backstreet). Drs. William and Suluka Holmes—the first male and female African American doctors in Fort Valley—partnered to operate a tin shop, theater, and drugstore with H.J. Jordan and a blacksmith with Gideon Barnette. Barnette also opened the first funeral home for African Americans here. Also located on this street was Harris Shoe Shop, Willis Hollinshead's shop, and Nathan Byron's restaurant.

Looking east, the same buildings are shown around 1970. The first building was used as Wilson Galleries and an American Legion hall. Further down was Moncrief Grocery, Pepper's Grocery, Sutton's Grocery, and Boyington House. Wilson Galleries store moved in the 1980s next to Bassett Hotel in what was originally Watson's Boarding House (also known as the Commercial Hotel). The Bassett Hotel, owned by Stephen Hicks Bassett, burned on June 21, 2006. (Courtesy of the *Leader-Tribune*.)

This c. 1916 life-size display is an advertisement for Chero-Cola, a cherry-flavored cola. A 1919 business directory indicates J.W. Pass operated Chero-Cola from "upstairs" in the Masonic hall on Church Street. Chero-Cola and Coca-Cola were still operating as separate businesses at that time. An interior view of the Chero-Cola Bottling Company around 1916 is below. (Both, courtesy of Helen Rhea Luce Stumbo.)

Coca-Cola Bottling Company was located next to the Bassett Hotel on West Church Street for at least 30 years before building a facility in the 1930s on North Macon Street. In the early 1900s, Fort Valley prohibited the selling of Coca-Cola on Sundays within city limits. The "new" Coca-Cola Bottling Company was a brick structure with stone pediments and stone signage bearing the familiar logo script. Eventually, the bottling activities ceased in the local facility, and it was used as a storage and distribution center. It was demolished in 2012 to make way for a fast-food restaurant. (Courtesy of W.C. Wyatt.)

Originally, this was the Dorsey Hotel, owned by early Fort Valley settler Mathew Dorsey. By the 1860s, it had become the Planter's Hotel. There are accounts from men having eaten at the Planter's Hotel before boarding the train that would carry them to join the Civil War. Some time later, as indicated by an 1881 business card, its name changed again: "Nice, clean, cool rooms at the Dixie Hotel." This building on the west side of the railroad tracks was built in response to the prosperity to be had with freight and passenger rail business. By 1911, Fort Valley had a population of 3,000 people and offered convenient service for rail travelers in the presence of hotels, boardinghouses, and restaurants. The 1920s marked the peak of railroad operations. The second story was lost to fire in the early 1970s, when it was part of Lowe's Hardware Store. (Courtesy of Helen Rhea Luce Stumbo.)

Facing Railroad Street, J.F. Lowe Hardware & Grocery Store was started in 1904 by John Fletcher Lowe Sr., who had been principal at a Wellston school. Lowe had a reputation for having anything a farmer would need, from dry goods to horse collars and pistols to dynamite. He was joined by his son J.F. Lowe Jr., who ran the store until his death in 1973. (Courtesy of Wilmetta Langston.)

In this photograph, taken in the early 1950s, the passenger depot is on the right; note the raised covered platform and the "water filler" for the steam locomotives. The water tower and smokestack from the city utilities building rise above the Winona Hotel, behind the switching tower. To the left of the palm trees is Happyvale Flour Mill and Anthoine's Machine Shop. (Courtesy of Marion Allen.)

The former Central of Georgia passenger depot, built in 1900 on Lowe Street (also called Railroad Street) and East Main Street, is one of three railroad buildings in Fort Valley. Large paired wooden brackets accent the eaves of this building. The mammoth wooden doors on the depot lift straight up, utilizing wheels and pulleys. Since its service days, this building has housed a variety of business offices, restaurants, and shops—one being Valley Insurance, owned and operated by the Holly family, which celebrated its 75th anniversary in 2012.

The two-story Switching Tower–Signal Building, at the corner of Main and Railroad Streets, was constructed around 1910. Prior to the electronic method, trains were switched using manual controls that necessitated this building. On the ground level was a restaurant for the tourists. The second floor was used as a telegraph office. Since its service days, this building has housed a variety of business offices, restaurants, and shops. (Courtesy of Walter Haussner.)

The freight depot was the first of the railroad buildings constructed. Having the switching tower, passenger depot, and freight depot makes Fort Valley one of the few communities in Georgia with all three buildings intact. The first train came through Fort Valley in 1852. In the late 1860s, Fort Valley was the No. 1 cotton-producing area in Georgia. Reconstruction, the peach industry expansion, and a variety of other agricultural produce sent to northern markets merged with other events to set Fort Valley's economic future. Entire trainloads of peaches in refrigerated cars left Fort Valley regularly, bound for destinations around the nation. Later, shipments of sand from the Atlantic Sand Co. were added, keeping the freight depot busy.

Over the years, a number of rail lines have serviced Fort Valley. In return, Fort Valley has offered the best of Southern hospitality to its travelers. When the first passenger train arrived on August 16, 1888, it consisted of the locomotive, baggage and mail car, and two passenger coaches. The *Flamingo* passenger train made its last stop in Fort Valley in 1963. From the front steps of the Winona Hotel, one could look east and see J.H. Hale's farm orchards three miles away. (Courtesy of Riley Kinney.)

In 1881, Henry Clickett Harris built the Harris House Hotel—it was later known as the Winona Hotel—in red brick with white wood trim on Main Street facing the railroad tracks. Harris was a major stockholder in the Atlanta & Florida Railroad. Unfortunately, he lost his fortune when the railroad bankrupted in 1887. George David Hartley, a farmer, merchant, and businessman, purchased the Harris House (pictured above) and renamed it the Winona Hotel for his granddaughter Winona Pearson, as seen below. Several businesses were located at the street level, including Lister's Barber Shop, which became Richard Scallon's Barber Shop, and the Candy Kitchen. Anyone who lived in the area between 1913 and 1965 has a memory of the Candy Kitchen (known as Pete 'n' Gus's). It was known for its hot dogs, fountain Cokes, and delectable candy made on the marble counter tops. Many have tried—without success—to duplicate brothers Pete and Gus Wouvis's secret hot dog sauce, a recipe they took to the grave. The Winona Hotel was torn down in the late 1960s.

The H.V. Kell Building was constructed around 1912 as a chain grocery-hardware-wholesale store that served the Middle Georgia area. Note the stenciled advertising that was used extensively in the 19th and early 20th centuries but rarely survives today. It also housed Hart's Nursery and the Peppercorn Restaurant at one time. It is currently owned by the FVSU Foundation. Serving the same purpose, B.T. Marshall's Grocery Co. was one block over; that building has since been demolished. (Courtesy of Marilyn Neisler Windham.)

It is not known if this log cabin stood here, at the intersection of Main Street and Commercial Heights, when the Troutman House was moved closer to the railroad tracks or if it was built later. Nor is it known when the structure was removed. It may have been used by John F. Troutman Sr. when conducting his farming and freight business. John F. Troutman Jr. did use it as a real estate and insurance office. Later, it was part of Doddridge K. Houser's Gulf gas station. The log cabin can be seen in photographs of the 1920s Peach Blossom Festivals.

Sam and Kay Hardeman Meyer stand in front of the family business, Jolly Nut Company (also known as Wright and Solomon), founded in 1924. In the 1940s, it was purchased by Wallis B. Hardeman Jr., whose daughter Kay Hardeman Meyer is currently at the helm. She and her late husband, Sam A. Meyer Sr., and their children, Sam "Lynn" and Katherine, as well as various other family members, represent three generations that have worked at this, the second oldest company in Fort Valley. Known today under its trademarked name of Jolly Nut Company, it is recognized for its signature pecan products. This structure was built in the late 1800s and once housed a steam engine–driven gristmill. It was also home to a Texaco oil business and served as a cull house for a peach-packing shed located in an adjacent building. (Courtesy of Kay Hardeman Meyer.)

Anthoine Machine Works, established in 1885, is the oldest continuously running business in Fort Valley. Records indicate that in 1904, in addition to machine work, Anthoine's carried coffins, caskets, and burial robes. Today, Anthoine's fabricates parts for industries and farmers. It is one of the only machine shops in Georgia using line shafts. Anthoine's is a treasure trove of old catalogs and ancient hardware finds. (Courtesy of the *Leader-Tribune*.)

This is Main Street looking west toward the post office at the end of the street in the 1950s. Seen on the right are Harrison Brothers, Avera Rexall Drugs, and Edwards Clothing. On the left are a coffee shop, the Candy Kitchen, Armstrong's, Jordan Electric, Liberty Café, and the Peach Theatre.

Harrison Brothers in the 1960s slowly phased out of the grocery business, with the exception of the big red Coca-Cola machine in the back of the store, adding televisions and appliances to its inventory as demand increased. In those days, televisions were like pieces of furniture, and almost as much attention was given to the appearance and quality of the wood cabinets as to the quality of the picture. In the 1940s, prior to Ralph and Holmes Harrison acquiring the grocery store, it was owned and operated by Heard Bartlett. (Courtesy of the *Leader-Tribune*.)

William and Fefie Khoury arrived in Fort Valley in 1936 and opened their first store, Khoury's Department Store, selling ready-to-wear clothing in this location. Loraine Turner Khoury and her four-year-old son William Khoury III are standing in front of the original location as it looked in 1971 with its 1949 facade remodel still in place.

Khoury's Department Store expanded by combining the old store (pictured above) with the two adjoining stores, Carither's Furniture Store and the Fashion Shoppe. A new sign and facade was done in 1972. It was one of the few stores to survive the tornado in 1975. The men's store moved across the street in 1987. After the ladies' store closed, Rent-a-Center, then Aaron's, occupied this location. The Khoury family—William Sr. and Fefie, William Jr. and Loraine, and James and Cheryl—have had five clothing stores since 1936. The third generation—William III, Alex, Chris, Natalie, and Andrea—contributed to the family business as child models, gift wrappers, and sales clerks.

Pictured is an interior view of Anderson Drug Co. around 1936. From left to right are Malcom Taylor, Homer Avera, Ben Anderson, Bunch Haslem, and Roy Rowland. The company was started in 1870 by proprietors Mathews and Green. It was sold to W.C. Wright and his son William M. in 1885 before ownership was turned over to Ben Anderson and Homer J. Avera in 1924. The drugstore operated under the name Anderson Drug Co. until Anderson's death in 1941, then the trade name became Avera Drug Co. (Courtesy of Gary Sheffield.)

Avera Drug Co. was Fort Valley's oldest business and the oldest drugstore in continuous operation in Georgia until it closed in 2011. The drugstore was in business for 141 years. Several pharmacists worked and trained at Avera's, including Louise Avera Peterson, C.W. "Pete" Peterson, W.P. "Bill" Hopkins, Troy Whatley, Roy Gilbert, Gordon Smith, and Gary Sheffield. Sheffield was the last and sole owner at the time of closing. Like several other professionals before and after him, Dr. Willis Webb, an ophthalmologist during the 1950s, had his office above the drugstore. (Courtesy of the *Leader-Tribune*.)

Thomas Edwards owned and operated Edwards Clothing Co. as shown around 1945. Later, Par-San Men's Store moved from West Church Street to this location. Par-San was originally established with a ladies' store in 1950 by Jessie Parham and Lillian Sanders. Note the large glass showcase windows indicative of the modern styling growing in popularity. (Courtesy of Nick Strickland.)

The Kendrick Building, pictured around 1947 at the corner of Camellia Boulevard and Main Street, was the site of the 64 Tire Company. Note the gas pumps and where a customer could drive in for service. Later, it was closed in for Taylor's Drug Store. Ellie Bramblett Adams had the Blue Plate Restaurant behind 64 Tire Company and Taylor's. Later, she moved it to Five Points, making room for the first Par-San Men's Store.

Taylor's Drug Store is pictured as it appeared around 1952. For 21 years, from 1949 to 1970, local pharmacist Malcolm Taylor, known as Dr. Taylor, ran Taylor's Drug Store at the corner of Camellia Boulevard and Main Street. Taylor had worked at the Anderson Drug Co. The original Southern Bell telephone office was located above Taylor's Drug Store. Fort Valley's prefix was TA5 (825), which stood for Taylor5, and was assigned due to the exchange office location.

Kent and Bonnie Bonner Wirsing, a husband-and-wife pharmacist team, were the owners and operators of Wirsing Drug Store for 22 years from 1970 to 1992 at the corner of Camellia Boulevard and Main Street. In 1992, they built a pharmacy next to the Piggly Wiggly grocery store at Five Points. When the 1975 tornado came through downtown, it took off this roof, exposing Futral Surveying and attorney Tom Garwood's offices. Papers were scattered over pastures for miles. All of the merchandise in the front window, including watches and cigarettes, were blown onto the street, and a car landed in the store after coming through a side window. (Courtesy of Kent and Bonnie Bonner Wirsing.)

Rogers Grocery occupies the first story of the Masonic temple, constructed in 1897. The Masonic order meets upstairs. During the Civil War, it was used as a Confederate hospital. The ground level of the Masonic building was rented for a variety of businesses over the years, including McConnell's Five and Ten, Squire Restaurant, Little Star Grocery, and the law offices of Adams and Adams. Young's Superfoods, Paul Friedman Clothing, and the bowling alley were all located to the left of the lodge. Kempers and Rogers were combined to make room for the new, larger Colonial Grocery.

The Georgia Agricultural Works building is shown as it appeared in the 1940s. In the late 1800s, it was one of Osborne H. Miller's enterprises. The letterhead from 1871 reads, "Miller, Brown, & Co.—Proprietors of the Georgia Agricultural Works, Manufacturers of and Dealers of Fine Buggies, Carriages, Plantation Wagons and Agricultural Machinery." In April 1920, it was purchased by Lummus Machinery Co. of South Carolina. It was also the site of Mathews Furniture Co. and A&P Grocery. In the late 1940s, T.A. McCord's funeral home—complete with a chapel and an elevator to take one upstairs to select a casket—occupied this corner. Current owners Wilton and Ann Walton have operated Fox Valley Printing from here since 1985.

This site on South Macon Street is the humble beginning where Nick Strickland Sr. started Strickland Grocery & Hardware in August 1939 "with 3 cases of Coca-Cola." "Big Nick" expanded his Coke business by selling candy, snuff, individual cigarettes, chewing gum, and other snacks purchased from Timberlake Wholesalers. The store was created in an alley and was rented for 50¢ per week. (Courtesy of Nick Strickland.)

As Strickland's business grew, Strickland Grocery & Hardware moved across the street to this location. "Little Nick" joined his father and ran the business until 1989, a total of 50 years in four locations. The Stricklands rented this building from Charles Evans and later bought the building to its left. Another father-and-son hardware store team, Harry C. Reddick and son "Buddy," owned and operated Reddick Hardware across the street for many years. (Courtesy of Nick Strickland.)

In the foreground is the Evans Building at the corner of Camellia Boulevard and Main Street. It is a three-story brick commercial building constructed around 1902 by Albert Evans, a local peach farmer and businessman. It has been the site of countless businesses and professional offices over the last 100 years, such as C.R. Williams' Barber Shop, Dr. Daniel Nathan's medical practice, Houser and Lee Insurance, the Thomas Library, the post office, the Red Cross, Georgia Fruit Exchange, L. Carter Insurance, Dr. Nance (dentist), Postal Telephone Co., Southern Brokerage Co., C.L. Shepard (attorney), and A.C. Riley (attorney). Fort Valley had a library of record prior to 1878, and it has occupied several locations over the years.

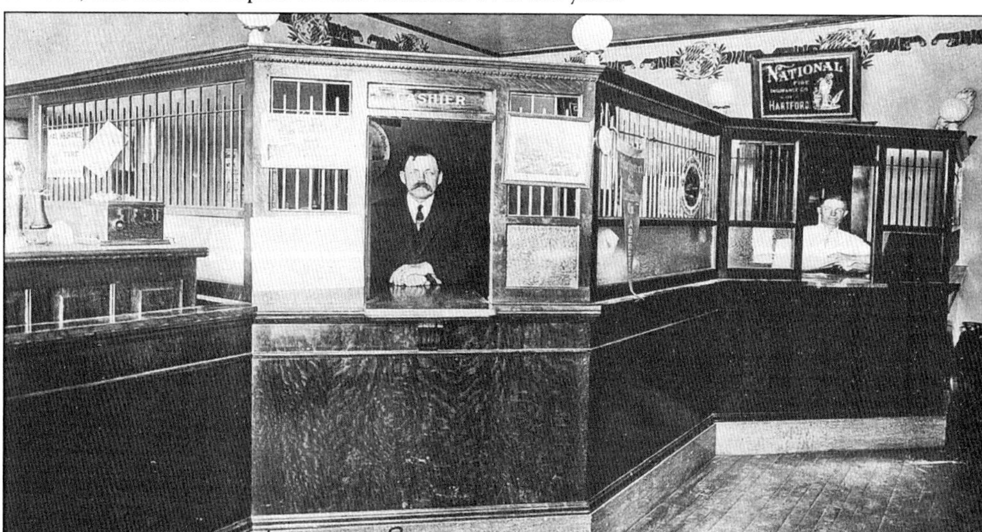

The Evans Building was the site of more than one bank operation, including the Bank of Fort Valley, Citizens Bank, and Middle Georgia Bank. There have been many changes in the banking industry over the last 100 years, as can be seen here. Leaded glass transoms and fanlights retain the letters "CB," marking the occupancy of past tenant Citizens Bank. The Evans family gifted the building to FVSU in 1997.

Pictured is an early location in the Evan's Building for Elrod's Five and Ten, which would later move a few doors down Main Street. Elrod's had everything from a candy counter to socks to Christmas trees. It was also the place to buy a Mother's Day gift or Easter basket.

George Bacon Culpepper Jr. was born in Fort Valley in 1899, became a lawyer in 1924, and practiced until his death in 1972. Culpepper is seen here at work on the second floor of the Evans Building with his secretary, Susie Delma Mathews Hutto, in the 1920s. It was the beginning of the family business, as both his son (George Brown Culpepper) and grandson (George Bryant Culpepper) are also attorneys. (Courtesy of Carole Hutto Odom.)

Seen here in the 1960s is Fort Valley's downtown, where three major routes (Georgia 49, Georgia 96, and US 341) intersect at the Triangle and again at Five Points. The streets still accommodate two-way traffic. The Holly Tree stands in Fincher Park. To the right on the corner in the Woolfolk Building is Wheeler's Drugstore, owned by L. Walstein and Elsie Rainey Wheeler and operated with Jim Nutt and Sue Markie. Walstein became a pharmacist in 1930. Markie worked the soda fountain, where she was famous for making milk shakes, floats, and other treats. It was the place to get a favorite comic book and hang out with friends. J.T. Ricketson bought the store and changed it to Ricketson's Drug Store in 1971. (Courtesy of Freddy Greer.)

In 1945, Herbert Jewelers was founded by D.N. and Mary Herbert, former schoolteachers who saw the potential for a fine jewelry store in Fort Valley. They started in this modest location in the Evans Building. It took 10 years before the Herberts found a suitable empty building to relocate their business on Main Street. Pictured here from left to right are Mary Spencer Herbert, D.N. Herbert, and Charles Holton. (Courtesy of Dennis and Peggy Childree Herbert.)

D.N. Herbert stands in his newly remodeled store at 104 Main Street in May 1970. For 40 years, son Dennis and his wife, Peggy, were the mainstay of the business until it closed in January 2010 after 65 years of business. Daughters Jana (Anthoine) and Lauren (Senecal) did everything from cleaning windows and counters to selling crystal and diamonds. Lauren's daughter Jasmine became the fourth generation to work in the family business. (Courtesy of Dennis and Peggy Childree Herbert.)

Shown is an exterior view of Elrod's Five and Ten in 1959. "Cleve's" is reflected backwards in the display window. Cleve's was a clothing store across the street that was owned and operated by Cleve Johnson. Johnson's Department Store was three doors down, owned and operated by Cleve's father, T.C. Johnson Sr. After Elrod's went out of business, it became an Allied Department Store and then Citi Trends.

Dora Sackellares, behind the counter, and her husband, "Chris" (Chrest), owned the Liberty Café (also known as Fort Valley Café and Chris's Café), located on Main Street from the 1930s to 1965. The Sackellareses would not sell hot dogs because they did not want to compete with the other Greek family in town, brothers Pete and Gus Wouvis's Candy Kitchen.

Par-San Men's Wear is seen as it appeared before the tornado in 1975. Businesses operating from 120 Main Street since the 1930s have been the Liberty Café, Par-San Men's Wear, and Khoury's Men's Wear. From 1965 to 1987, brothers Tommy and Terry Parham ran the Par-San Men's Store from this location. Since 1987, it is the site of Khoury's Men's Store, owned and operated by brothers William and James Khoury. The Khoury family has had several clothing stores in the downtown area for more than 76 years, spanning three generations.

Pictured is Main Street looking west as it appeared in late 1975, a few months after the tornado. There are signs in the windows, but signage on the buildings has not been replaced yet. Stores include Habersham Music, City TV, Recreation Pool Hall, Jordan Electric, Par-San Men's Wear, Cato's, Christopher's Furniture, Herbert's Jewelers, and Stripe Department Store in the Evans Building. (Courtesy of Freddy Greer.)

The Odd Fellow Hall Historical Marker reads, "On this spot in 1866 stood a 2 story building known as the Blind Academy. It housed the first school for Black Children in Fort Valley. Also what is now Usher's Temple C.M.E. Church met here for services during that same time. Out of the school came the Fort Valley High and Industrial School which is now Fort Valley State College. The building was demolished in 1989."

Chapel Hall was the first school building constructed on the Fort Valley State College campus and was later destroyed by fire. In the background is the first model school that was built, also lost to fire. Dr. Donny D. Bellamy's *Light in the Valley* is the authoritative history of FVSU.

In 1929, the Academic Building was constructed with funds contributed by the general education board and friends. The first Ham and Egg Shows were held in the Academic Building, renamed Founders Hall in 1976 to honor all the founders collectively. It was part of Fort Valley High and Industrial School, eventually becoming Fort Valley State University in 1996.

Carnegie Hall was built with funds from the Andrew Carnegie Foundation in 1925. The library was on the second floor. It has been used as the administration building and the campus security center. Henry A. Hunt and Florence Johnson Hunt are entombed in front of Carnegie Hall. A plaque listing the original 18 founding members is next to their graves.

Built in 1932 as a post office for $60,000, this Classical Revival structure exceeds the usual decorative elements of government buildings. Corinthian capitals with Wedgewood insets accent the limestone columns. The cornice features green and gold detailing, and the fanlight, with egg-and-dart molding, is accented by green, blue, and peach inlay work. The granite steps lead to a lobby of pink Georgia marble. It has been repurposed as the Fort Valley Police Department.

The 1936 Peach County Courthouse, built by the Works Progress Administration, and the 1932 post office were constructed in the eastern portion of the residential district where it blends into downtown. Originally, the second floor of the Austin Theatre served as the courthouse. The 1936 structure was partially destroyed by a fire in 1969. At that time, the Thomas Public Library was housed in the south end of the building, and it sustained the most fire damage. It was renovated in the early 1970s after the fire and again in the 1990s. The courthouse sits on the site of the Fort Valley Female College, chartered in 1860.

As early as 1886, Fort Valley had a public school called the Grady Institute located at College and Miller Streets. It was named for Henry W. Grady of *Atlanta Journal* fame. In 1895, there were 100 students enrolled. To enter a college or university, one had to pass written examinations.

This park-like area has been known as the Schoolyard, Church Square, and Beauty Square, and now it is called Everett Square. James Abingdon Everett, founder of Fort Valley, and Mathew Dorsey, a fellow land speculator, gave six acres to the trustees of the Fort Valley Academy in 1836 for the purpose of building a school and a church. The academy was built in 1848. Prof. W.J. Scroggs was a well-known teacher and principal who had two sons. Will was an editor for *Encyclopedia Britannica*, and Phil was an architect who designed the first Fort Valley public school built on Everett Square. The new building seen here, Fort Valley High School, was occupied in 1912 with grades one through 11 under the leadership of Supt. Dr. Ralph Newton. (Courtesy of Helen Rhea Luce Stumbo.)

The 1927 Academic Gothic Revival–styled Fort Valley High School at the edge of the Everett Square Historic District faces Knoxville Street. The street was paved to the end of the school property, and the rest of it was a dirt road. The Westview section did not exist at the time, nor did Highway 96. The only way to get to Reynolds was to go to Roberta on the Old Atlanta Highway. Brick bungalows and minimal traditional cottages of the same era surround the school. FVHS was home to the Green Waves until 1974. Anderson field (named for Supt. Ernest Anderson) was directly behind the building. It now houses the board of education offices.

Fort Valley Methodist Church, founded in 1835, was known as the Old Pond Methodist Church. It was originally located on the Old Atlanta Highway (US 341). In 1848, the congregation built a new church on Everett Square. The congregation sold that property and built this sanctuary on the corner of Miller and West Church Streets in 1936. (Courtesy of Helen Rhea Luce Stumbo.)

Usher's Temple C.M.E. Church on Railroad Street was originally known as Usher's Chapel in 1866. It was the first "free" church for African Americans in Fort Valley. Members worshipped in a building on O'Neal Street known as the Blind Academy and later as Edward's Funeral Home. The upper floors were used for worship, and the ground floor was the first school for African American children. From these humble beginnings came the Fort Valley High and Industrial School, St. Peter's A.M.E. Church, and Shiloh Baptist Church. Rev. J.H. Usher was the first ordained elder and pastor. The first church constructed on this site burned in 1880. The present building was erected in 1959.

The First Baptist Church (Fort Valley Baptist Church until 1964) stands on the corner of College and Miller Streets and was organized in 1852 with seven members who met twice a month in a downtown warehouse. The first church building burned in 1935. The congregation met above what is now the Austin Theatre and in the Strickland Hardware Company building until 1947. Fort Valley Baptist Church sponsored two churches: the Second Baptist Church (which later became Chamblee Memorial Church) and Society Hill Church. (Courtesy of Helen Rhea Luce Stumbo.)

According to oral tradition, Shiloh Baptist, as a congregation, started in 1863 on Union Hill under a bush arbor (as did St. Peter A.M.E. in 1890). Shiloh had both Baptist and Methodist pastors. In 1870, Joel R. Griffin, for whom Griffin Line is named, gifted "one-half more or less land" to Caroline Felder, Randall Rutherford, and Peter Slappey as trustees. Two members of Shiloh were among the 18 founders of Fort Valley State College: Rev. Peter Fann and Thomas W. Williams Sr. In 1912, Trinity Missionary Baptist Church was organized by 35 Shiloh Baptist Church members. (Courtesy of Homie Regulus Heritage Collections and Archives, Henry A. Hunt Memorial Library.)

St. Luke's Episcopal Church's Historical Marker reads: "This parish had its origins in the Episcopal Church's support of Fort Valley High and Industrial School in 1913, which it operated from 1919 until 1939 in partnership with the American Church Institute for Negroes in New York, the Diocese of Atlanta, and the Diocese of Georgia. In 1939, the school became Fort Valley State College and part of the University System of Georgia. Fort Valley College Center became St. Luke's Episcopal Church in 1958. Through a gift from New York philanthropist Ethel Mary Cheney Thorne, the current building was designed by Stanislaw Makielski and constructed in 1939–1940." (Courtesy of Homie Regulus Heritage Collections and Archives, Henry A. Hunt Memorial Library.)

St. Juliana Catholic Church was built in 1953 and dedicated in 1954. Rev. James H. McCown, S.J., who helped lay the brick, stands in front. The site on US 341 was selected because it was a main thoroughfare for northern tourists, and Catholic churches were rare in the South. Prior to the church being built, Sunday masses were held in the homes of William and Fefie Khoury (1937–1954) and Dr. Waldo and Josephine Blanchet. Dr. Blanchet became president of Fort Valley State College in 1966. In 1980, a major addition of classrooms and a fellowship hall was started; it was completed in 1981.

St. Andrew's Episcopal Church was established in 1880, when the first Episcopal missionary was assigned to Fort Valley. Parishioner George Harrison, a cabinetmaker, built the first chapel in 1897. Timbers from the original chapel were used in this 1920 structure on Central Avenue.

Fort Valley Presbyterian Church was established in 1872 with 14 members. Services were first held in a local hotel before this 1916 structure was built on Central Avenue. The front doors, framed by a rounded pediment and semicircular stained-glass fanlight, create a welcoming entrance through the corner steeple. The Reverend S.S. Gaillard was the organizing minister.

Rev. Stephen Elisha Bassett founded the Congregational (Methodist) Church in the late 1880s on the corner of Miller and Persons Streets. Soon after the 1969 courthouse fire destroyed a large portion of the library, a new Thomas Public Library (dedicated in 1972) was built on this site. It has since been repurposed as the 911 center and courthouse annex.

Three

Parades and Celebrations

Fort Valley loves to celebrate its people, holidays, and of course, the peach. Many types of parades and celebrations have emerged over time. Festivals, parades, celebrations, firework displays, and other special events contribute to the quality of life in a community. Their importance is universal, transcending cultures and time. Parades have also become a means to bring awareness, protest, and inform. They provide people with a sense of belonging and camaraderie as well as entertainment.

A parade has become an important part of Fort Valley's Christmas tradition and Santa's arrival. Parades also mark special events, people, and celebrations such as the Georgia Peach Festival, Fort Valley State University's and Peach County High School's Homecoming celebrations, and returning veterans.

When one hears Felix Mendelssohn's "Wedding March," he or she is transported to another time and place. Watching the synchronized movements and hearing the marching band play are an important part of the celebratory atmosphere of a parade, too.

Graduation and award ceremonies are not only rites of passage but often memory milestones, as is hearing Sir Edward Elgar's "Pomp and Circumstance March No. 1." There is nothing quite like the experience of moving one's tassel from the right to the left. The recognition awards bring, and the associated feelings of approval, acceptance, and appreciation, can change lives.

The following images are glimpses of many parades and celebrations long past, although the traditions continue.

From 1922 to 1926, Fort Valley attracted as many as 50,000 visitors to the "peach capital of the world" and the Peach Blossom Festival each spring. The teepees in the center background indicate the location of pageant activities. Nearby, for two days, 600 men barbecued 400 hogs over six pits, a total of 600 feet in length, for festival visitors. This photograph was taken at the intersection of East Main Street (US 341) and Oakland Heights (also called Possum Trot or Commercial Heights). Marilyn N. Windham's *Peach County, The World's Peach Paradise* is devoted to the history of the Peach Blossom Festivals.

Costumed characters in the festival pageant production ride in a horse-drawn wagon. At first look, it appears to be one of the parade floats. Every member of the cast had to pay for his or her own costume. Reportedly, some of the more elaborate costumes used satin, silk, brocade, and rhinestones and averaged $500 each.

This view looks down (probably from a Harris House Hotel window) on a Peach Blossom Festival parade as it travels Railroad Street. The New Dixie Hotel is on the left, the passenger depot is on the right, and the Bassett Hotel and Coca-Cola Bottling Co. can been seen at the end of the street to the right. Many elaborately decorated floats and marching bands from all over Georgia representing businesses and communities were entered in the festival parade.

The *Atlanta Constitution* reported that the 1926 Peach Blossom Festival attracted more than 40,000 visitors. People watched the festivities from their windows and rooftops. The elaborately decorated float representing Byron, also in the newly formed Peach County, leads the way down Main Street. It is followed by Atlanta's Technological High School Band. The crowd makes it difficult to see the telegraph office on the left. Across the way, facing Church Street, Georgia Agricultural Works, Peach Poultry Company and Hatchery, Georgia Grocery, Miller Furniture Company, Green-Miller Company, and Rogers Grocery can be seen. Among the 1926 guests was a Hollywood film crew. Unfortunately, all known copies of the resulting movie have been lost or destroyed.

To honor or acknowledge the local veterans as part of an event was an important tradition. Confederate veterans gather in front of the Masonic lodge in downtown Fort Valley around 1910. Many letters exchanged during the war between Capt. S.G. Pryor and his wife, Penelope T. Pryor, have been edited by local attorney Charles R. Adams Jr. and published as *A Post of Honor, The Pryor Letters 1861–63.*

Shortly after Operation Desert Storm in Iraq ended in 1991, local soldiers from the US Army Reserve gather for a victory parade commemorating their return and honoring those who lost their lives in the conflict. Fort Valley Main Street's Everett Square Park Committee, chaired by William Khoury, raised funds to create a multifunctional park that includes a walking path and a veterans' memorial. Robert Spinks of the American Legion, Ann and Linda McGehee, Walter Lanter, Peggy Herbert, and others worked with Peach County commissioners Tom Palmer, James Khoury, Joe Collins, Walter Smith, Martin Mosley, County Administrator Marcia Willis Johnson, the public works department, and Billie Seagers to make a number of improvements. Local author Billy Powell included a list of World War I and World War II veterans in his book *Echoes from the Valley.* (Courtesy of Kent and Bonnie Bonner Wirsing.)

Chief Grady C. Cochran stands in the middle of the intersection of Main, Church, and Macon Streets across from Fincher Park directing traffic as the town anxiously waits for the parade to begin. It was 1947, the first year the Fort Valley High School Green Waves fielded a band. This photograph was taken from the Evans Building. Cochran was chief of police for more than 34 years. He helped start the Georgia Association of Chiefs of Police and was its first president. (Courtesy of Nick Strickland.)

The FVHS Green Waves Marching Band is performing in 1947 in front of Little Star Grocery. From left to right are majorette Joyce Murphy, Betty Becham, majorette Claire Houser, Ann Monk, majorette Norma Young, Joan Barfield, majorette Maxine Hatchet, and Betty Sue Allen. (Courtesy of Nick Strickland.)

The 1960 FVHS Green Wave Majorettes preformed colorful and entertaining halftime shows with the band during the football games. Standing on the steps of the Green Waves gym are, from left to right, Frankie McDaniel, Gayle Vining Wells, Kay Hardeman Meyer, Cherry Dupree Maughon, Gwenndoln KenKnight Hallman, Ann Saywell Spears, and Betty Ruth Edwards.

The Fort Valley State College Wildcats Marching Band is pictured on Main Street in a Christmas parade. On the left is Christopher's, Elrod's Five and Ten Store, and the Evans Building before crossing Georgia 49 (also called Macon Street or Camellia Boulevard). On the opposite corner is the Woolfolk Building, which was home to several businesses, including Wheeler's Drug Store (later Ricketson Drug Store) and the Robert E. Lanyon Law Office. (Courtesy of Homie Regulus Heritage Collections and Archives, Henry A. Hunt Memorial Library.)

Reportedly one of the world's most recognized people, World Heavyweight Champion Muhammad Ali was the grand marshal of the 1989 Fort Valley State College Homecoming Parade. That year, Ali was also on the cover of a special *Sports Illustrated* issue celebrating his 35 years in boxing. (Courtesy of Dorothy Myers Crumbly.)

Saundre' Brown, the 1975–1976 Miss Fort Valley State College, and two attendants ride the parade float as it travels down South Macon Street. Brown grew up in Fort Valley and was a speaker at the FVSC centennial program during the 1995–1996 homecoming celebration. (Courtesy of Dorothy Myers Crumbly.)

Annette Church, Miss Hunt High, is driven by her father, Robert Church, in a late-1970s parade. H.A. Hunt High School was officially established with the construction of a new school building located on Spruce Street in 1954. (Courtesy of Dorothy Myers Crumbly.)

Miss Tiger Sweetheart and an attendant are second-grade students at Hunt Elementary School, seen here riding in the Hunt High pageant parade in November 1967. From left to right are the driver, agriculture teacher James Gibson; attendant Rita Edwards; and Miss Tiger Sweetheart Valerie White. (Courtesy of Elizabeth Harris White.)

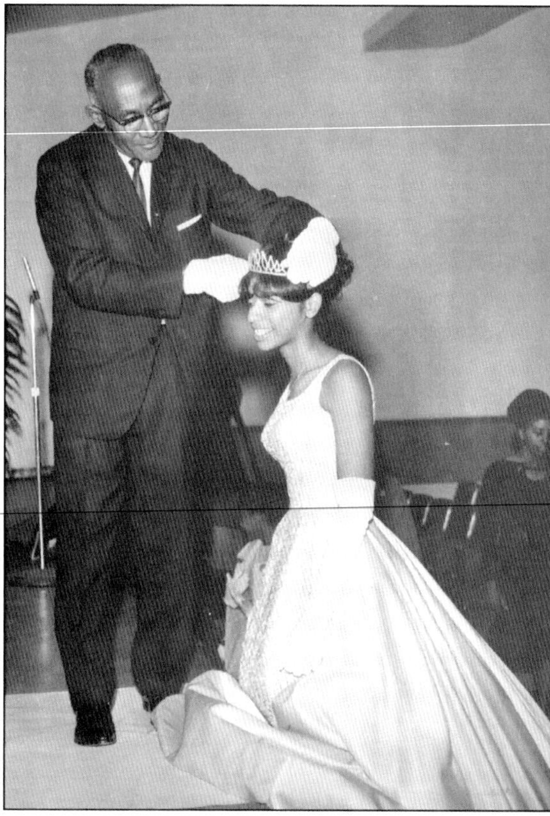

Principal H.E. Bryant crowns the 1966–1967 Miss Hunt High, Beverly Anne Delton. Her father, Col. Thomas Delton, built the first subdivision located on what is now called State University Drive, naming it Beverly Hills for her. (Courtesy of Elizabeth Harris White.)

Stacy Sheffield, the 1994 Peach County High School Homecoming Queen, and her father, Gary Sheffield, a local pharmacist and businessman, are pictured during Homecoming celebrations. She carried on a family tradition as Homecoming royalty—her mother, aunt, and niece were queens, and her father was a Homecoming king. (Courtesy of Gary Sheffield.)

Beverly Mobley and Elaine Lewis carry the banner for an early Peach County High School Trojan Band some time around the mid-1970s. Note the Sears building on the right; it was later Yoder's Gym. During the flood of 1994, the roof collapsed under the weight of rainwater accumulation.

Blue Bird Body Company's costumed bluebird leads the way for the 1927-built "Blue Bird No. 1" bus in Fort Valley's Christmas parade. Eventually, Blue Bird No.1 was retired from parade duty, and in 2008, it was donated to the Henry Ford museum in Dearborn, Michigan. Blue Bird No. 1 was built on a Ford chassis.

Santa Claus rides atop a horse-drawn wagon in the 1912 Christmas parade. Two traditions have survived the decades of Christmas parades in Fort Valley: no matter how the route may be altered from one year to the next, the parade always finds its way downtown, and a Christmas parade would not be complete without an appearance from Santa. The Lions Club sponsored the Christmas parades for many years. Seen below, Santa Claus arrives atop a 1925 LaFrance. It was purchased new and brought in on a railcar. It is still in service at the time of this writing. Firefighters are, from left to right, Otis Daniels, Chief Lewis Maye, and Tony West. (Below, courtesy of Jeff Doles.)

The *Nancy Hanks* excursion train replica would participate in the Halloween or Christmas parade. The local *voiture* (boxcar) or unit of the Warner Robins American Legion 40&8 La Société was the sponsor. The real *Nancy Hanks* excursion train was named after a racehorse that was named after Abraham Lincoln's mother. (Courtesy of the *Leader-Tribune*.)

"Don't talk about a farmer with your mouth full" was written on a sign hung from a tractor in the 1979 Tractorcade, in which 6,000 family farmers drove tractors to the Mall in Washington, DC, to protest farm policy. (Courtesy of the *Leader-Tribune*.)

The first day of issuance of the Camellia Stamp (April 23, 1981) was a significant event in Fort Valley's history. On this day, stamps honoring the camellia and three other flowers was issued for the first time at the post office on Anderson Avenue. The Fort Valley Post Office received that distinction because it serves the National Headquarters of the American Camellia Society, better known as Massee Lane Gardens. On hand for the occasion was former president Jimmy Carter, who was present at the ceremony held at the post office and at Massee Lane Gardens. It cost 18¢ to mail a letter in 1981.

Massee Lane Gardens' Southern Belles were a Camellia Festival and Flower Show tradition for many years. From left to right are Gladys Pearson, Laurie Pearson, Evelyn Webb, Vergie Jones, Dottie Godwin, Muriel Nathan, Lena Belle Duke, Annette Duke, Mac Pearson, Carolyn Sammons, Julia Adams, Nonie Wilson, Diama Smith, and Jamie Pearson, with Dave Strother and Maxwell Murray in the back.

Pictured is the ground-breaking for the FVHS Green Waves gym around 1948. The gym had wooden bleachers and seated 600. It is still in use today by the Peach County Recreation Department. From left to right are (first row) two unidentified, Felton Hatcher, Billy Wood, Bill Wilson, and Mayor T.A. McCord; (second row) Lucile Rodgers, Alice Woods, unidentified, Mildred "Miki" Kendrick Mathews, three unidentified, Betty McGee, Lawton Pearson, and two unidentified; (third row) William Khoury Sr., two unidentified, Wallis Hardeman, Newt Jordan, T.A. Jones, Supt. Ernest Anderson Sr., George Wheaton, and Bennett Rigdon Sr. (Courtesy of the *Leader-Tribune*.)

The ground-breaking for the Peach County High School Trojans gym was held around 1974. Pictured from left to right are Asst. Supt. Henry E. Bryant, architect Stan Adams, Peach County Board of Education member Clarence Davis, Supt. Earnest Anderson Sr., Peach County Board of Education member Joe Johnson, Peach County Board of Education member Ed Dunbar, an unidentified contractor, and Peach County Board of Education member Billy Dick. (Courtesy of the *Leader-Tribune*.)

The Fort Valley High School Junior and Senior Proms in 1959 and 1965 reflect the changing times. Notice the difference in dresses and hairstyles made in just a few years. The floor-length 1950s Cinderella-style gowns would have been pink, powder blue, or yellow and made of lace and tulle with silver rhinestones. To complete the princess look, the gowns were complemented by the white arm-length gloves and faux-gemstone necklaces. By 1965, the gowns included those shortened to below the knee and made from silk organza over silk taffeta and lined in China silk, as shown here.

Attending a banquet at H.A. Hunt High School are teacher Ruby Church, county agriculture agent Robert Church, and Principal Henry E. Bryant (standing). The Peach County Chamber of Commerce named an award for outstanding service in education in Bryant's honor. (Courtesy of Dorothy Myers Crumbly.)

This photograph captures a Fort Valley State College Founders' Day presentation. From left to right are Leon "Stan" Lomax, head football, basketball, and track and field coach; Isaac Miller, son of Houser A. Miller, who served as registrar (and a relative of the college's founders); FVSC's third president, Dr. Waldo W.E. Blanchet (1966–1973); and Dollie Bea Dixon Horton, director of college and community relations.

Dressed in formal attire, these distinguished gentlemen are in the Fort Valley Woman's Club, at the corner of Church and Anderson Streets. Purchased in 1958, it was redecorated and had air-conditioning installed; the clubhouse now served the community as a convenient and attractive place for civic, social, and private gatherings. Pictured from left to right are Wilbur K. "Punk" Avera, Jack Hunnicutt, unidentified, Tom Anthoine, and David Sammons. The Fort Valley History Club was established in 1904 with Mrs. Louis L. Brown (Cornelia Hartsfield) as president. It expanded its mission and became the Fort Valley Woman's Club in 1924.

Fort Valley firefighters' sweet treat of homemade peach ice cream has been a tradition since the 1920s, thanks to the generosity of 38-year veteran volunteer fireman Gus Wouvis. Wouvis donated the 10-gallon reclaimed freezer, and Lts. Eddie Hannon and Clinton Hutto fashioned the churn's motor. In 1996, the Fort Valley City Council Fire Committee of Marvin Crafter, Norman Fitzgerald, and N.W. Jordan commended Chief G.L. Moye and Capts. Autry Little and Otis Daniels for publishing the first history of the Fort Valley Fire Department. From left to right are Newt Jordan, Eddie Hannon, Ted Jones, and Lewis Moye. (Courtesy of Todd Bryan.)

The Peach Blossom Festivals are gone, but in 1986, the first Georgia Peach Festival was staged. In addition to the abundance of great food, music, and entertainment, the Kiwanis Pancake Breakfast, a 5K road race, golf tournament, and other events have been added to the county-wide event held each June, along with arts and crafts vendors. The world's largest peach cobbler—measuring 11 by 5 feet and using 75 gallons of peaches—is made each year. Sissy Jones initiated it, and the tradition was continued by Matt Mullis, Rich Bennett, Jan and Tim McCord, and others. Pictured around 1994 are, from left to right, Susan Luckie Youngblood, Hank McCord, Molly McCord, Tim McCord, Linsey McCord, Jan Luckie McCord, and Roy Miller. (Courtesy of the McCord family.)

Shown is the ribbon-cutting ceremony for the 1974 Golden Anniversary of Peach County celebration headquarters office on Main Street. This space had been Armstrong's Department Store; later it was Calvin Mason's City TV. In 1978, Anne S.K. Jefferson's ASKA's Discount Beauty Supply opened there, and it operated in this location for more than 25 years. It is currently the site of Beth Cleveland's Peach Palette. From left to right are Joe Chapman, three unidentified, Cleon Moore, Freddy Greer, two unidentified, Bill Alford, Claybon Edwards, Latrelle Alford, Billy Dick, unidentified, Lovie Newberry, unidentified, Laurie Pearson, Donnie Doles, two unidentified, and Durwood Gassett. (Courtesy of Freddy Greer.)

The 1976 Bicentennial celebration had a performance by the Peach County High School Glee Club members wearing patriotic red, white, and blue dresses that they made themselves. They were led by Patsy Thomas. Pictured are, from left to right, (first row) Richard Dennis, Gena Cleveland Ray, unidentified, Sandy Yuhas, and Lisa Lanter; (second row) Mary Elizabeth "Liz" Adams Johnson, two unidentified, Jeannie Webb, and Bobbi Kim McHale; (third row) unidentified, Carole Anne Cato-Edison Hice, unidentified, Linda Bartlett, and Cathy Aultman Dobbins; (fourth row) unidentified, Ellen Futral Hanson, Tammie Gallmon Ellerbee, Billie Shepard Joiner, and Ellen Gassett.

The year 1887 is the date written on this photograph of the Fort Valley Concert Band. Band members are standing in front of Harris House Hotel on Main Street. The golden age of bands, from the mid-1800s to the 1920s, was characterized by each community having its own volunteer band.

Georgia's 77th governor, George Busbee (1975–1983), signs a proclamation for Fort Valley State College Day in Georgia in 1975. From left to right are Frank Dean Martin III, Leon Hollinshed, unidentified, FVSC president Cleveland W. Pettigrew, Governor Busbee, Dollie Horton, Eugene Odom, and Ralph Malone. (Courtesy of Frank Dean Martin III.)

Georgia's 76th governor, Jimmy Carter (1971–1975), is pictured with a Peach County delegation. From left to right are Ed Dent (city council); Sheriff Reggie Mullis; Mayor Paul Reehling, Claybon Edwards (city council); Wilbur Spillers (city council); Governor Carter; Rep. Dan Grahl; M.L. Gilchrist (Fort Valley city administrator); David Parker (city council); Rudolf Carson (city council); Donnie Doles (county commissioner); Charlie Adams Jr. (Fort Valley city attorney), Tom Franklin (county clerk), Ray Anthoine (Fort Valley city clerk), and Sen. Ed Barker. (Courtesy of the *Leader-Tribune*.)

Baccalaureate speaker Rev. Dr. Martin Luther King Jr. meets students and guests on June 5, 1966. In the background is the historic Anderson House. From left to right are Dr. William Lyder, dean of graduate studies; Fort Valley State College's first lady, Katye Murphy Troup; Dr. King; Fort Valley State College's second president, Dr. Cornelius V. Troup (1945–1966), and three unidentified guests. (Courtesy of Albert O'Bryant.)

Four

Familiar Places and Faces

As Wilson Rawls writes in *Where the Red Fern Grows*, "It's strange indeed how memories can lie dormant in a man's mind for so many years. Yet those memories can be awakened and brought forth fresh and new, just by something you've seen, or something you've heard, or the sight of an old familiar face."

Investing oneself in a place is what gives meaning to it. It is the places where one does something special, often with friends, colleagues, and teammates, where one acts, creates, performs, finds, changes, and grows, or even falls in love, that become special, memorable, or even magical. Places and faces do matter.

The common desire to seek the familiar is instinctual. As people grow older and experience loss, the drive to connect or reconnect is like an infant to his or her parent. Seeing those familiar faces and places brings back the memories, the stories of times past—and often a sense of security, comfort, and belonging—just as it has for those who go before and those to follow. The story behind some of these photographs may surprise some. Many will awaken the nostalgia, sentimentality, or whatever one wishes to call the desire to share and reminisce.

The people in the following pages could be elected officials, local legends, or not. They are a small representation of the people who operated businesses; served on the library or school board; led a troop of Girl Scouts or Boy Scouts; were presidents of the garden club, Kiwanis, or other club; headed the chamber of commerce; taught school; lent a hand in community theater productions; or volunteered at church. Literally thousands of residents were influenced by these generous and talented people. These are the very people who get things done in a small town, and they are the people who often get left out of the history books—to all, we are grateful.

This prominent four-story structure was known as Happyvale Flour Mills. It made cornmeal, flour, grits, and animal feeds under the labels Happyvale (flour and cornmeal), Pure Joy (flour), and Pay Day (dog, cat, hog, horse, cow, and cricket feed). Happyvale began operation in Fort Valley in 1934 with owner Clyde Nichols from Griffin. By 1955, his son Bill owned and operated Happyvale; it closed in 1983. Across the tracks from downtown on East Main Street (US 341), Happyvale was flanked by Woolfolk Chemical Works and Anthoine's Machine Shop. This photograph appears to have been taken from the water tower.

Along with the agricultural economy came a demand for chemical fertilizers and pesticides. Woolfolk Chemical Works manufactured agricultural chemicals adjacent to downtown Fort Valley and next door to Happyvale Flour Mills to fill the demand. The pesticides were produced under the Security brand name. Woolfolk was later bought out by Canadyne Corporation. It is now the Marion Allen Insurance Company headquarters.

In the 1980s, the Environmental Protection Agency discovered that the ground around the Woolfolk Chemical Plant was contaminated, and steps were taken to correct the damage. US EPA Region 4 presented Fort Valley and the Woolfolk Alliance its Excellence in Site Reuse Award for working together and returning a Superfund site to beneficial use. The Superfund Redevelopment Initiative, started in 1999, cited Fort Valley for its important role, pioneered by the community and Mayor Dr. John Stumbo, in the reuse planning process now utilized across the country.

There were several residential homes lining both sides of Highway 341, known as Main Street at the time and Martin Luther King Jr. Drive today. Several homes on the east side of 341 were removed as a result of the Woolfolk (Canadyne) cleanup, and the new Thomas Public Library was constructed on some of the remediated lots. Completed in 1998, the Thomas Public Library—Peach Public Libraries system headquarters—has the additional distinction of being a national model; it is the first Superfund redevelopment in the state of Georgia and the first public library built on a Brownfield site.

Edwards Funeral Home was started in 1929 by Martin Edwards. In 1945, son Andrew "A.J." joined his parents in the family business. Claybon also joined his brother and parents in 1963. Eventually, it became C.J. Edwards Funeral Home, with Claybon as president and chief executive officer, and Edwards Insurance Agency was added. Edwards was the first African American elected to the Fort Valley City Council in 1970. He served for 12 years, two of them as mayor pro-tem. (Courtesy of Wilmetta Langston.)

Holland's Court Motel opened in the 1930s. A postcard description from the 1950s reads, "Phone 340. Steam Heat—Refrigeration Air Conditioning. On Routes U.S. 341—State 7 (Also Short Cut on U.S. 41 Barnesville to Perry, Ga.) Approved By Duncan Hines, AAA." This was the main route to Florida prior to Interstate 75. Before World War II, "the older kids" would go out to Holland's and dance to the jukebox. Farther down was NeSmith Truck Stop, now the site of Hick's Funeral Home. NeSmith, like Thurman's Truck Stop, was important because local produce and crops were moved by truck from farm to market and to and from the railroad.

John Fletcher Lowe Jr.'s recall for an item in his cramped store was legendary. Stuffed full, the sounds of wooden floors, and the scent of everything from candy to fertilizer—that was Lowe's. Railroad Street was renamed Lowe Street, and a park on Miller Street was named in his memory. (Courtesy of Nick Strickland.)

Inside the old post office are familiar faces of longtime postman Julian Jones and local businessman Wallis B. Hardeman of Jolly Nut Company in the early 1970s. The post office was on the corner of Anderson Avenue and West Church Street. It has been repurposed for the Fort Valley Police Department. (Courtesy of the *Leader-Tribune*.)

Blue Bird Body Company is shown as seen from the air in 1977. Blue Bird was founded in 1927, when a friend asked Albert L. Luce Sr. for a bus to transport his workers. His request gave Luce the opportunity to create the first Blue Bird school bus. It spearheaded the beginning of a highly successful corporation. Blue Bird has grown to be the world's largest school bus manufacturer. (Courtesy of the *Leader-Tribune.*)

Blue Bird Body Company was founded and grew successful by building buses completely out of steel. During World War II, due to government restrictions and the scarcity of metal, several changes were made, including using tongue-and-groove pine for the bus floors. Blue Bird also held government contracts to build ambulances in support of the war effort. On an unusually cold winter morning in 1945, this plant caught fire after coal was added to a heating stove. Once the fire reached the paint room, it spread quickly as the paint cans exploded. Less than 45 minutes after the fire was discovered, the wooden structure had collapsed. (Courtesy of the *Leader-Tribune.*)

Albert Luce Sr., pictured in No. 1, makes an "L" for Luce. The Luce family played a major role in the history of Fort Valley, as Albert Luce's three sons—George, "Buddy," and Joe—took over Blue Bird and guided it to a position of prominence. The Luce brothers sold it. Blue Bird No. 1 was sent to the Henry Ford museum in Michigan in May 2008. Luce had used a steel body instead of wood and incorporated a Ford Model T chassis in the 1927 Blue Bird No. 1. (Courtesy of Clayton Luce.)

Pictured here are the employees at the Bank of Fort Valley on January 7, 1977. From left to right are (seated) Wynelle Wingo, Marge Pierce, Jo Cobb, Brenda Sanders, Emma Thomas, Retha Ezell, Connie Davis, and Beth Morton; (standing) Lavenia Scott, Fred Glenn, Nita Irby, Helen Batton, Lucy Becham, Jackie Taylor, Bobbie Woodruff, Ronnie Middlebrooks, Maxine Byrd, Lew Culpepper, Zelma Smisson, Karen Fogg, Lynn Hodges, Ray Anthoine, Julie Layfield, Carole Odom, Jerri McDaniel, Billie Patterson, Shelia Bennett, Willie Owens, Melanie Watson, and William H. "Bill" Elliott. (Courtesy of Carole Hutto Odom.)

Citizens Bank, originally chartered in 1906 in Marshallville, moved headquarters to Fort Valley in December 1963. Citizens Bank operated in the Evans Building and an old depot before building on the Smissons' peach shed site near Five Points in December 1979. There, Citizens Bank celebrated its 97th year. (Courtesy of the *Leader-Tribune*.)

Citizens Bank employees are pictured here around 1977. From left to right are (kneeling) Durward Gassett, Judy Holland, Sara Middlebrooks, Betty Mason Vining, Betty Hamlin, Andrea Tucker, Barbara Matchman, and Betty Woolfolk; (standing) Freddy Greer, Waverlyn Collins Grant, Fran McCord, unidentified, Diane Mullis, Nancy Kocher, Bertha Adkinson, Carol Bryant, Sarah Young, Patsy Sutton, Paula Pender, Myleen Barfield, and William "Bill" Huckabee. (Courtesy of Freddy Greer.)

The 1947 Green Waves Marching Band majorettes stand at parade rest in front of Fort Valley High School, unseen on the right. In the background, Park's Grocery faces the intersection of Knoxville and Vineville Streets. At that time, Vineville Street (Georgia 96) was a dirt road. The Westview residential section was undeveloped farmland. Pictured from left to right are majorettes Joyce Murphy, Norma Young, Claire Houser, and Maxine Hatchet. (Courtesy of Nick Strickland.)

Park's Grocery Store was a familiar sight well into the 1960s, especially for those who attended Fort Valley High School. Hattie Parks would bring her wares of Cokes, honey buns, and other sugary delights to the edge of campus for students who were not permitted to cross the street during their lunch hour. After school, Park's Grocery was a favorite meeting place for neighborhood kids, who bought their baseball cards, Cokes, chips, bubble gum, and other snacks from this grandmotherly lady. (Courtesy of Kent and Bonnie Bonner Wirsing.)

Located just north of the intersection of Persons and North Macon Streets (Georgia 49) was Curtiss Singletary's Sing Oil station, pictured about 1947. Sing Oil Company was a small South Georgia oil company, one of many at the time. There was a bus stop in front where many returning World War II soldiers disembarked. The brick building on the left was Williams Motor Co., which was owned by Herschel V. and Rosa Mathews Williams and their children, brothers Francis and Herschel V. Jr. They sold Pontiacs and Buicks. The house of Clara Passmore, a Khoury's employee for more than 30 years, is seen on the right. The station was torn down for Williams Motor Co. parking. By 1978, the house was torn down to make way for a fast food restaurant. From left to right are J.W. "Bill" Hudson and R.E. Schofill. (Courtesy of the Peach County Historical Society and the Hudson family.)

Yates Crutchfield's Texaco service station is pictured around 1953 on North Macon Street between the Ford Motor Co. and Holland's Standard Oil service station. Crutchfield purchased the station from Felton Hatcher. Before Interstate 75, there were 31 full-service gas stations and three truck stops in Fort Valley. The attendants would wash the windshield, pump the gas, check the oil, and more for a fraction of a dollar per gallon. They also carried multiple fuel grades for automobiles, kerosene, and distillate, which tractors ran on before diesel. (Courtesy of T.J. Crutchfield and family.)

Fort Valley, the peach capital of the world, was located on the main route to Florida, and a number of service stations and motels flourished before the advent of Interstate 75. This Union gas station, owned by Garnet Pirkle, was located at Five Points. Prior to it being a Union station, it was a Pure Oil station. This building was later removed to make way for a fast food restaurant. (Courtesy of the *Leader-Tribune*.)

Connie Hall bought this property in 1931 for $49.20 from the Fort Valley City Council and started a service station. The dinosaur, a Sinclair gasoline symbol, was affectionately called "Alfred." Connie's wife sent postcards (more than 5,000) to tourists who had stopped there. Her practice resulted in a large repeat tourist business. They were open 24 hours a day, seven days a week, because of the high volume of tourist traffic headed to Florida. (Courtesy of Sarah Hall Eliassen.)

Dick Rhuling's Hall's Half Acre was considered a state-of-the-art service station in 1966. Attendants checked tires, oil, and fluids and cleaned the windshield as they pumped gas for customers. The redbrick building in the background was the chamber of commerce. It was originally the home of Blue Goose Brokers for the peach industry. The white two-story structure was Pearson's Packing Shed, one of three located next to each other on Vineville Street. It was later destroyed in a fire. After Hall's was torn down, it was an empty lot until around 2005, when an automatic car wash, Chevron self-service gas station, and convenience store were constructed. (Courtesy of Sarah Hall Eliassen.)

Albert Miller's Sinclair service station is seen with his niece Joyce Miller Key, her husband, Donnie Key, and Philip Robinson in the background. Miller's Service Station was located on South Macon Street (also called State College Drive and State University Drive) just as one crosses the railroad tracks. Apartments are there now. (Courtesy of the *Leader-Tribune*.)

M Supply Company, established by Ernest McGee in the old Ford Motor Company location on Macon Highway, moved to this site on the Marshallville Highway (Georgia 49) in the 1950s. M Supply now deals in lumber and building materials, including paints and varnishes and plumbing and electrical supplies. The building was constructed by J.D. Duke to store his supplies and equipment for peaches in the summer and pecans in the fall. Its design is unique in that there are no interior support beams. The roof is supported by arches. (Courtesy of Betty Parham McGee.)

Pictured is Habersham Funeral Home, located on South Macon Street (also known as University Drive), as it looked in the 1970s. Trinity Baptist Church is on the left. Habersham Funeral Home was first known as People's Funeral Home. In the 1930s, Henry A. "Hal" Hunt Jr. bought it and renamed it H.A. Hunt Funeral Home. His son Charlie operated it into the late 1970s before Earnest and Mae Habersham purchased the business. It burned in 1995—a total loss. (Courtesy of Wilmetta Langston.)

Carter's Foodtown, on State College Drive, was owned by David "Dave" Carter. He was also the owner of Carter's Construction Company, and he created the Willow Lake subdivision. Carter was the first African American appointed to the board of education and elected to the Peach County Board of Commissioners. (Courtesy of Albert O'Bryant.)

Albert O'Bryant purchased Carter's Foodtown, and after significant renovations, he renamed the convenience store Community Plaza. O'Bryant also owns Cool 'N' Dry Storage and shares his business experience as an adjunct professor to a number of universities. (Courtesy of Albert O'Bryant.)

The C.W. Pettigrew Farm and Community Life Center was dedicated in 1987 on Fort Valley State College's campus as an outreach to the community. It is a conference, convention, and fine arts facility. It was named in honor of Dr. Cleveland W. Pettigrew, the fourth FVSC president (1973–1982).

Displayed are cured meats, fresh eggs, and canned produce in the 34th annual Ham and Egg Show. County extension agent Samuel Otis O'Neal started the famous Ham and Egg Show in 1916. The Ham and Egg Show idea spread across Georgia and the South. Agent O'Neal went to the African American farmers, whether they were renters or owners, to improve their family health and living as they cured their meats and raised their chickens and livestock. Margaret Toomer taught home food preservation techniques. Portraits of H.A. Hunt and John Davison, Fort Valley High and Industrial School principals, flank the display. (Courtesy of the Homie Regulus Heritage Collections and Archives, Henry A. Hunt Memorial Library.)

In 1982, under county agent Dr. Glenwood Hill, the Ham and Egg Show was revived as the Ham and Egg Breakfast. Giving farmers and other local people the opportunity to interact with their legislators, the Ham and Egg Breakfast evolved into an annual political, agriculture-based forum. Hill also served on the Peach County Board of Commissioners (1985–1993) and as its chairman.

Sam Nunn (from Perry, wearing glasses at right), a candidate for the US Senate, converses with Georgia representative Bryant Culpepper (Fort Valley). Nunn began his political career in 1968 in the Georgia General Assembly. In 1972, he won a seat in the US Senate, serving a distinguished 24 years until retiring in 1996. Culpepper served in the Georgia House of Representatives from 1975 to 1982 before succeeding his father, Judge George B. Culpepper, in 1982 by being elected to the Superior Court of the Macon Judicial Circuit. After serving seven terms, Culpepper retired in 2007.

The Fort Valley City Council members in the chambers are, from left to right, Clinton Hutto (firefighter), Escol Bennett (Western Auto Store), L.B. Knight, Mayor David Sammons (1964–1970; real estate), Newt Jordan (Jordan Electric), G.C. "Dud" Poole (Poole's Café), and William "Bill" Liipfert (Woolfolk Chemical Co.). Jordan was the longest-serving city councilman in Georgia—38 years at the time of his death. (Courtesy of Carole Hutto Odum.)

The Fort Valley City Council members in the chambers are, from left to right, L.L. Westmoreland (Economy Men and Boys Department Store), Bobby Hester (Bobby's Minute Mart), Claybon Edwards (Edwards Funeral Home), Mayor Paul Reehling (1970–1980; WFPM radio station), Rudolf Carson (insurance), Newt Jordan (Jordan Electric), and Robert Church (county extension agent). Edwards was Fort Valley's first African American councilman, serving from 1971 to 1982. His daughter Denise Edwards Small became the first African American female to serve on the Fort Valley City Council in 1996. (Courtesy of Dorthy Myers Crumbly.)

A "city council" convenes for coffee and conversation each morning, as seen in this c. 1978 photograph. Pictured from left to right are Doddridge Houser, Albert Evans, Charles Evans, Felton Hatcher, and Lynn Brown. The Governor Treutlen Chapter, Daughters of the American Revolution's *History of Peach County, Georgia* is the authoritative source for the family histories of early settlers, of whom these gentleman are all descendants. (Courtesy of the *Leader-Tribune*.)

This c. 1952 photograph of Fort Valley notables includes, from left to right, Marion Culpepper Wilson (Mrs. Z. Chester), Mary Spencer Herbert (Mrs. D. Neal), Irving Rigdon, Marion Allen, Dan Grahl, John Armstrong, and Col. B.A. Shipp. They represented the chamber of commerce, Kiwanis, American Legion, and Fort Valley Woman's Club. (Courtesy of Dennis and Peggy Childree Herbert.)

In the 1970s, there were few better known personalities in Middle Georgia than Fort Valley mayor Paul Reehling. Reehling was also owner and operator of WFPM radio. He raised Fort Valley from the debris of the 1975 tornado, which struck the heart of the city without warning. He left his mark on countless reconstruction and beautification projects such as new streets, sidewalks, lighting systems, and parks. He was elected to five consecutive terms as mayor from 1970 to 1980.

Robert Church (left), campaign manager, congratulates Rudolf Carson upon his election as mayor of Fort Valley. Carson served on city council from 1972 to 1980 and then went on to be elected Fort Valley's first African American mayor from 1980 to 1982. Church also served on city council from 1972 to 1982.

A visit by Bosnian library officials in September 2000 was sponsored by the US Department of State and the US Embassy and hosted by Peach Public Libraries (PPL). They were welcomed by more than 75 guests. Pictured from left to right are PPL director Gilda Stanbery, Byron city attorney Larry Collins, PPL director emeritus Jimmy Smith, Bosnian guests Slavica Hrnkas and Biserka Sabljakovic, PPL trustee Wilmetta Langston, PPL assistant director Ashley Moore, PPL trustees Elizabeth White and Ann Blair Brown, and Bosnian guest Tatjana Maric.

Kay Community Service Center, also known as the Kay School, provides a year-round sports program and work opportunities for adults with developmental disabilities. Pictured from left to right are Jack Brinkley, US representative from Georgia (1968–1982); Lena Belle Kay Duke; daughter Kris Duke; and an unidentified man. Kay School was cofounded by Lena Belle, Edgar L. "Junebug" Duke Jr., and Dr. Carlton Morse in 1960. It was named in honor of Lena Belle's parents, Dr. James Benjamin and Lena Kay of Byron. James Earnhardt was the director for many years.

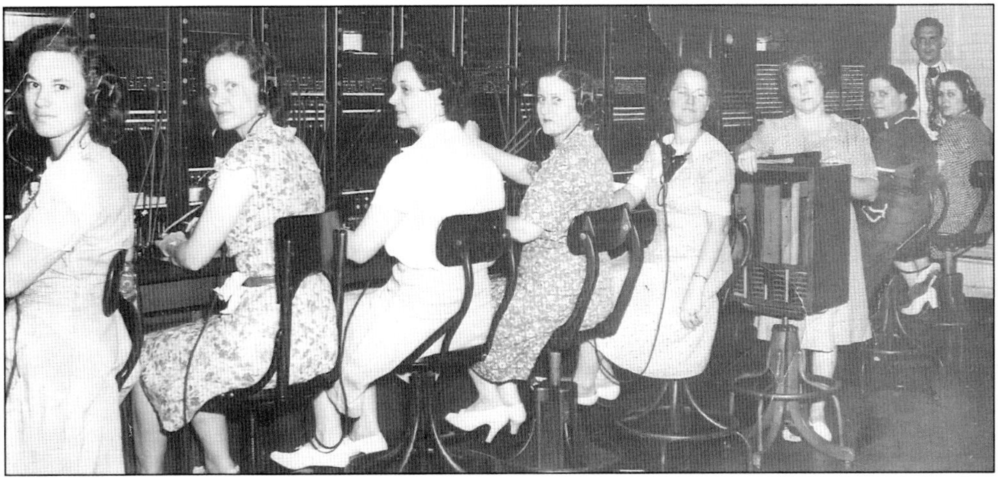

Around 1895, the Bell System adopted the standard "Number, please!" as the way to answer a switchboard. People called the operator by dialing "0" for all kinds of information—everything from the scores for that night's football game to why the lights were on at the funeral home. Operators in the original Southern Bell office above Taylor's Drug Store in the 1940s are, from left to right, Rose Marie White Pearson, Inez Wheeler, Dolly Silvey, Ruth Kemper, Maggie Dent, Bertha Bateman (chief operator), Estelle Hallman, Frances Wells, and Robert Wells. (Courtesy of Debbie Sandefur Spearman.)

Prior to May 1925, Fruit Belt Telephone Company provided Fort Valley's service. In 1976, employees gathered at the Southern Bell office on Anderson Avenue to celebrate the 100th anniversary of Alexander Graham Bell's invention of the telephone. Pictured from left to right are (first row) unidentified, Ben Day, Larry Tucker, Ken Hall, and Larry Hunnicutt; (second row) Mikki McPherson, Inez Ellis (seated), Katherine Clark, Margaret Moncrief, Wayne Johnson, Danny Sanders, Tommy Joyner, J.E. Brown, Verma Ellington, Debbie Spearman, Jane McCants, Dot Rowell, Agnes Mathis, Lois Spinks, and Jeri Lavendar; (third row) Ronnie Sanders and O.B. Brown. (Courtesy of Debbie Sandefur Spearman.)

In this 1985 photograph is a Chamber of Commerce First Dollar Bill ceremony and ribbon-cutting for Wilson Galleries with, from left to right, (first row) Bucky Wilson, Ann Stanley Wilson, Mayor C.W. "Pete" Peterson, James Khoury, Freddy Greer, Sissy Jones, Marlon Maddox, and Herman Stine; (second row) Jill Wilson, Stan Wilson, Patty Wilson Greene, Ernest Greene, Emory Wilson, Dr. Curtis Gene Waites, Dennis Herbert, Bill Huckabee. Wilson Galleries was not an ordinary furniture store. It had a staff of professional interior decorators and fine furniture showrooms drawing people from all over the state.

This is a c. 1980 ribbon-cutting for the Community Development Block Grant Housing Improvement office. Shown from left to right are program director Alfred Ellis III, Melanie Miller (city clerk), Robert "Bob" Church (Fort Valley City Council), Janet Hudson, Sandra Blasingame Smith, Rudolf Carson (Fort Valley City Council), and Robert Byres.

A 1966 *Vallihi* yearbook caption says it all: "The inmates in 'The Hole' take time to drink a Coke, eat a sandwich and shoot the bull." Pictured are, from left to right, (first row) Duke Lane, Tommy Smisson, Gary Barr, Wes Wheeler, and David Luckie; (second row) Jimmy Williams, Buddy Reddick, David Dunning, Randy Runyan, Jeff Liipfert, Bobby Lane, and unidentified; (third row) Austin Barnett, Bill Jones, Warren Young, and Buddy Marshall. (Courtesy of Debbie Dunning Liipfert.)

Marie Johnson Anderson receives the Star Teacher Award, presented by Durward Gassett at Kiwanis in the old American Legion Hall Post No. 76 in the early 1970s as an unidentified Star Student looks on. Anderson taught science in Fort Valley and Peach County public schools for decades, served as a library trustee for nearly 20 years, and was active in the Methodist Church.

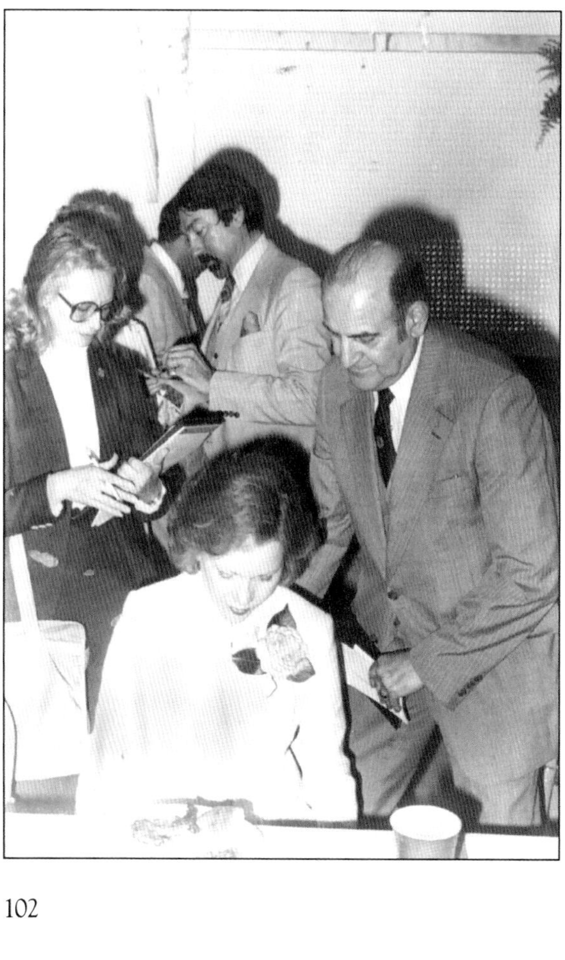

In 1994, the Key to the Library was presented to a library volunteer who had gone above and beyond. This photograph was taken in the Gena Riley Meeting Room of the Thomas Public Library on Persons Street. Eugenia Riley was director of the Thomas Public Library from 1927 to 1965. Peach Public Libraries trustees are, from left to right, Ann Blair Brown (PPL chairwoman and executive director of the American Camellia Society), Wilmetta Langston (teacher in Houston County Schools and FVSU Archives employee), and William "Bill" Alford (retired Peach County Schools administrator and Peach County commissioner, 1970–1974).

First Lady Roslyn Carter signs her autobiography, *First Lady From Plains*, for Dr. Dan Nathan in 1984. Her book signing was held at the American Camellia Society on the beautiful grounds of Massee Lane Gardens near Fort Valley.

Five

Ties That Bind

Fort Valley has been shaped by its unique cultural and historic heritage, including Native Americans; early European settlement by the English, Scots-Irish, and Scottish; the central role of agriculture in the antebellum economy; a stratified society according to land ownership; the importation of enslaved Africans; the presence of a large proportion of African Americans in the population; and the aftermath of the Civil War—all evident 150 years or more later.

It is a place where the people are socially conservative, have strong attachment to their community, love NASCAR and collegiate sports, maintain strong loyalty to family ties and their high school football team, and pass on Southern cooking from one generation to the next while preparing for Sunday dinners and church socials. Like most Southerners, the people in and around Fort Valley attend church on a regular basis. The churches are plentiful, influential, and highly visible.

The landscape is characterized by the sweeping live oaks, tall straight pines, flowering dogwoods, pecan and magnolia trees, crepe myrtles, fragrant jasmine vines, cabbage palms and palmettos, yards filled with roses, camellias, and azaleas, and, in the spring, acres and acres of peach trees in bloom.

The area's history is full of the seeming paradoxes of the people who belong simultaneously to traditional-minded organizations and to a variety of forward-looking associations that engage in impressive social reform. Often doing similar work for different reasons, both groups emphasize history, memory, and education with the potential to oppress as well as to help free.

Ties that bind are the common experiences residents share by growing up and living in a community and being a part of its culture. The collective history of the peach industry is firmly entrenched in Fort Valley, the county, and the entire state's identity. The ties that bind are the schools, libraries, and newspapers and the catastrophes, such as tornados, floods, fires, train wrecks, and murders, that are carried from generation to generation and become a part of Fort Valley's individual and collective identity.

The Hale brothers were one of the pioneer peach families. John Howard "J.H." and George were originally from Connecticut and owned about 2,000 acres in peach orchards and 1,000 acres called Hale Orchards in Fort Valley on Miami Valley Road, now Georgia 96 East. J.H. helped establish Storrs Agricultural College, known today as the University of Connecticut. This 1895 photograph shows the many hands needed to pick the fragile peaches. (Courtesy of Billy and Barbara Hale Davidson, Miami Valley Farms.)

"Hooker," "spooner," "jooger," and "turner" were names for the special people who work in packing sheds, along with "ringers," "fillers," "labelers," and "loaders," as seen in these 1895 photographs. (Courtesy of Billy and Barbara Hale Davidson, Miami Valley Farms.)

The largest operations included self-sustaining businesses to support peach farming, such as an on-site cannery or the crate and basket factory in this 1895 photograph. The baskets carried the fruit from the tree to the wagons in the field and then to the shed. There, the fruit was sorted and packed in crates before being sent to market via wagon, truck, or train. (Courtesy of Billy and Barbara Hale Davidson, Miami Valley Farms.)

At one point, more than 50 packing sheds ran during peach season around Fort Valley, providing thousands of jobs for young and old alike and creating an almost insatiable demand for refrigerated railroad cars. (Courtesy of Billy and Barbara Hale Davidson, Miami Valley Farms.)

Oakdale Cannery was owned by Dr. Josiah A. Flournoy. In 1861, Flournoy purchased a small plantation about three miles outside of Fort Valley, located at the railroad bridge on the old Marshallville Road and settled by Reuben Slappey. The farm was noted for its fine old residence and a beautiful collection of fruits and flowers. (Courtesy of June Preston See.)

Each farm had to depend on itself, and 50 acres were devoted to the house gardens for the Flournoy family. Every home, large and small, had its own orchard and grew many varieties of fruits. The peaches were mostly cling-stone for pickling and preserving. Red, yellow, and blue damson plums, apricots, and cherries were also canned. (Courtesy of June Preston See.)

John Pearson is seen dumping a box of peaches onto a peach filler inside of Pearson-Lane Packing Company. Two prominent peach families merged to have a joint packing shed located on Highway 341 North. The Pearsons operated under the label of 4 J's, which stood for Joe, John, Jimmy, and Jane Pearson Hulbert. Lane's was founded by John David Duke in 1908 and operated under several names: Lane Packing, Pearson-Lane, Southern Orchards, and Lane Southern Orchards, its current name. The Lane family moved into their current location on Highway 96 East in 1990. This facility has become a tourist destination, with over 300,000 visitors each year. It currently employs the fifth generation of the family. From left to right are Joe Pearson, John Pearson, and Jody Jackson.

Ask anyone who grew up in Fort Valley, and he or she will tell a story about "working in peaches." Working in peaches meant long, hard hours, but the money was worth it. Seen here are workers sorting apples once grown around Fort Valley. Another crop that has declined in prominence is asparagus, grown at the beginning of the 20th century. Asparagus can still be seen growing wild along the roadsides of Fort Valley today. Pecans have steadily grown to become the largest orchard crop in Peach County. Georgia is the largest producer of the 17 states that grow pecans. Several fruits, such as strawberries, kiwis, and blueberries, are also grown in the area.

From the late 19th century through the mid-20th century, the architecture and the downtown environment changed when building owners improved facades with new awnings to replace shed canopies. The *Leader-Tribune* was formed in 1888 when two newspapers merged, the *Fort Valley Leader* (owned by Thomas Virgil Fagan and edited by Samuel "Bully" Austin) and the *Fort Valley Enterprise* (co-owned and edited by Will Kersh and Will Wynne). The first newspaper, the *19th Century*, was published in the 1850s.

The 1921 graduating class was the first Fort Valley High School graduate class. There were 11 grades at the time. Pictured from left to right are (first row) Maude Wilson, Jo Allen, Ruth Spillers, Maymaie Ousley, Louise Gordy, Emily Avera, Annie Dee Wilson, and Myra Moskovitz; (second row) Idelle Bryant, Ruby Lawson, Mary Grimes, Bernice Fielder, Elizabeth Everett, and Pauline Carter; (third row) Albert Evans, Lewis Green, Ralph Braswell, D.R. Houser, Claude Wilson, and Sam Peddicord; (fourth row) teacher James Lovett Graham, Joe Graham, Louis Rigdon, Prof. Ralph Newton, Marion Vining, Kimbrol Smith, Jack Rundell, and Charles Baldwin. This photograph was taken on the steps of the original Everett Square school, first occupied in 1912.

Fort Valley High and Industrial School won its first state football championship in 1929. Pictured here are the Hunt High Tigers, who won the 1958 state football championship. Pictured from left to right are (first row) Little Son Hosley, Sonny Maddox, George Marshall, Doug Williams, Leroy Waters, ? Dixon, and Pap Howard; (second row) Jimmie Rucker, Doug Mathew, William Jordan, Willie William, Henry Marshall, Robert Smart, Willie Rucker, and Sol Lowman; (third row) Coach Merritt, Prof. H.E. Bryant, Tick Clark, David Hiley, Ernest Brown, Fred Horton, George Lightfoot, B.T. Thompson, Samuel Holloman, Floyd Keen, and head coach Lawrence Coleman. (Courtesy of Elizabeth Harris White.)

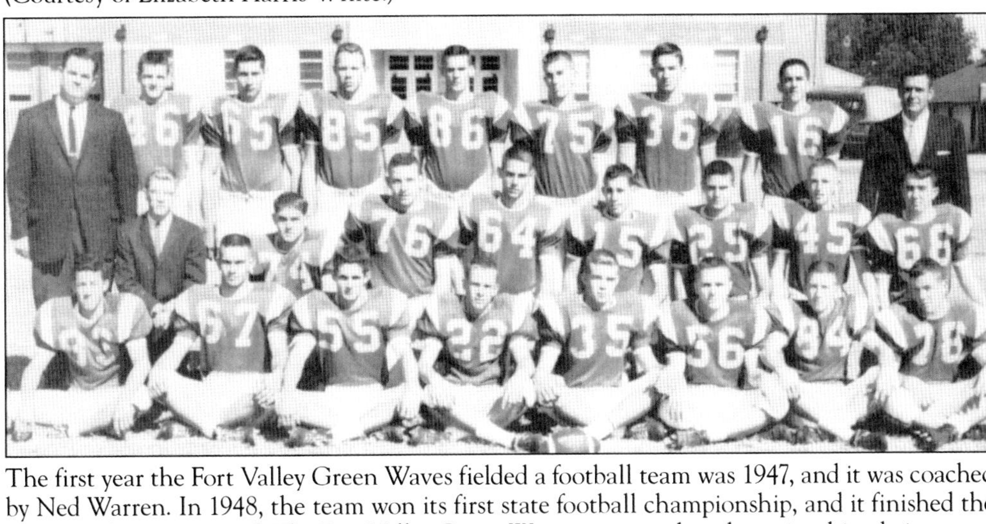

The first year the Fort Valley Green Waves fielded a football team was 1947, and it was coached by Ned Warren. In 1948, the team won its first state football championship, and it finished the season with a 12-0 record. The Fort Valley Green Waves won another championship, their second and last, in 1961 with a 13-0 record. They are pictured here in front of the gym. From left to right are (first row) Tommy Tucker, Jimmy Giles, Johnny Bradshaw, Jody Hardeman, Dan Harelson, Phil Mullis, Rodger Nelson, and Eddie Robinette; (second row) manager David Thompson, Thomas Greathouse, Johnny Walker, David Joyner, Dave Hardeman, Warren Wall, Ronnie McDaniel, and Al Bickley; (third row) head coach Norman Faircloth, Richard Lawhorn, Hugh Barr, Rusty Tomlinson, Nim Thorpe, Charles Volson, Ray Pearson, Tee Faircloth, and assistant coach Charles Sims.

The first Peach County Trojan Band is pictured here around 1974. The Trojan Band, under the direction of Randolph Lindsey (1974–2004), was very successful in winning awards and was often recognized as one of the best in the state. It was not unusual to see the band compete alongside college bands. The band included a rifle corps, the Golden Girls drill team, and the flag corps. (Courtesy of Eileen Lovett Weber.)

The Peach County High School Golden Girls are on the field ready to perform their dance routines in 1999. The first Golden Girls routine was performed to the prerecorded theme of Hawaii Five-O under the direction of Debra Byrd (1974–1997). Shown are, from left to right, (first row) Katie Mathews, Heather Walton, Kim Grahl, and Erin Culpepper; (second row) Tiffany Grant, Ashley Bowden, Jessica Giles, Natalie Khoury, and Kristin Wilson; (third row) Tarie Howell, Krystal Hawkins, Jenny Chadwick, Jennifer Hudson, Erin Rowe, Melanie Walker, Andrea Manor, and Kelli James; (fourth row) Afton Ellis, Francesca Duncan, Katie Pearce, Laura Gilwreath, Andrea Khoury, Megan Armstrong, Christin Miller, and Sherri Warwick. (Courtesy of Andrea and Natalie Ridgewell Khoury.)

The Fort Valley High School Green Waves basketball team is pictured here in 1949. From left to right are (first row) Pheland Lowe, Jack Roland, Bobby Wilder, Norris Mullis, Billy Cannon, Gordon McDaniel, and Donnie Young; (second row) Stuart Wood, Charles Bartlett, James Hutto, Jack Swan, and coach Ned Warren. FVHS won several state basketball championships (1952, 1954, and 1961), as described in *Pride of the Panthers* by Billy Powell.

The c. 1973 girls' basketball team members were, from left to right, Felice Dyson, Valerie White, Gwendolyn Davis, Gail Riley, and Delores Collins. The presenter is unidentified. Fort Valley and Peach County always had highly competitive and successful girls' basketball teams that won regional titles. The girls' team played at 6:00 p.m., and the boys' basketball game would follow. Many girls did double duty and were cheerleaders for the boys' games. (Courtesy of Elizabeth Harris White.)

For a few years, the Peach County Trojans played in the old Fort Valley High School Green Waves gym. Inside the gym, a crowd supports the girls' basketball team around 1973. Fort Valley has always had highly competitive and successful girls' and boys' basketball teams. H.A. Hunt High School had boys' state championship basketball teams in 1954 and 1960. (Courtesy of Elizabeth Harris White.)

This is an interior view of Hunt Elementary School and students in the 1960s. The H.A. Hunt High School Historical Marker reads, "In 1953 and 1954 the buildings on this site were constructed for the Henry Alexander Hunt High School. This Black secondary school came out of a series of schools called Fort Valley High and Industrial School and then Fort Valley Normal and Industrial School. H.A. Hunt High School first began in 1941. . . . The school closed in 1970 when it was merged into Peach County School System with Fort Valley and Byron."

Hunt Elementary School students in the 1960s practice their music outside. Prior to the H.A. Hunt High complex, constructed in 1954, students attended classes in the Peabody Building and the Academic Building on the campus of Fort Valley State College. (Courtesy of Elizabeth Harris White.)

Pictured here are the 1974 Peach County Trojans baseball team. Coach Tommy Fibbe started baseball in 1972. From 1972 to 1982, the Peach County Trojans won over 80 percent of their games, including sub-regional and regional championships, and were state runners-up several times. From left to right are (first row) unidentified and Matt Mullis; (second row) Sonny Bailey and unidentified; (third row) Rich Hudson, Michael Sparks, Kim Woodruff, Darold McCrary, Jeff Willis, coach Tommy Fibbe, Willie Paul Smith, and two unidentified.

The Malibu's started as a high school garage band in 1964 and are still performing all over the state 50 years later. The band has had very few changes to its lineup but has also been called Sixpence, Nightlife, Boardwalk, Sensations, and Celebration. From left to right are Chris Smisson, Dennis Herbert, Wes Wheeler, David Luckie, and Eddie Byrd. (Courtesy of Dennis and Peggy Childree Herbert.)

Dairy Queen, Tasty Freeze, Dope Hill, and others are the places residents went and hung out with their friends before the game, after school, or on a date. Joyce Beeland Mullis Smith built, owned, and operated the Dairy Queen and was later joined by her children, Matt, Reggie, Jim, and Holly. Everyone looked forward to winning the game or a night out, because that meant a trip for ice cream.

Members of Zeta Phi Beta Sorority, Inc., are pictured at an alumni function. From left to right are Maggie Thompson (home economics teacher), Marion Bryant (math and science teacher), Ruby Church (elementary teacher), Frances Bell (principal at Hunt Primary School), and Harriet Tabor (principal at Hunt Elementary School). There can never be enough said about the importance of teachers in shaping students' lives, and the community owes them a debt of gratitude. (Courtesy of Dorothy Myers Crumbly.)

Fort Valley's Olympic Welcome Celebration and Spirit Day culminated with the arrival of torch bearers to FVSU stadium. A processional of 10 torch runners representing Peach County and the Rwandan Olympic Team were greeted by FVSU's sixth president, Dr. Oscar Prater; Peggy Herbert, the chairwoman of the Torch Relay Committee; and others. Fort Valley mayor pro-tem Jeffrey Holly proclaimed July 2, 1996, Fort Valley Olympic Spirit Day. The torch runners areAnita Ponder (left) and Merchant E. Singleton (right). On the stage are, from left to right, Jeff Holly, Oscar Prater, city councilman Marvin Crafter, Mayor John Ezell, Peggy Herbert, two unidentified, and Rev. Julius Simmons. (Courtesy of the Anita Ponder family.)

Fort Valley has produced many college and professional athletes. Charlie "Whip" Davis was born in Fort Valley in 1927. Davis began his career in 1947 in Atlanta at a textile mill where black and white baseball teams played each other every Fourth of July. He played for the Birmingham Black Barons until 1950, when he was traded to the Memphis Redsox. He played in the east-west all-star game at Chicago Michigan Park. He pitched second to Satchel Paige. While barnstorming, he played against Hank Aaron, Willie Mays, Jackie Robinson, and Larry Dolby, to name a few, in all-star games. (Courtesy of Gary Sheffield.)

In 1972, the Cardinals Little League team had an undefeated season. The team included Brantley Sims, Emmett Hill Slappey, Buddy Sims, coach Charles Sims, Roger Sims, Eddie Watson, Tim Wilson, Bobby Barnes, Jeff T. Watson, coach Merrill Wilson, and Dale Taylor. (Courtesy of the *Leader-Tribune*.)

The Warren Green Auto dealership sponsored this girls' softball team playing on Warwick Field in the 1970s. Shown are, from left to right, (first row) Pamalia Ricketson, Janet Barnes, Kathy Parham, Terri Holly, and Elizabeth Strickland; (second row) Elaine Strickland, Kim McCants, Joey Ware, Kim Vining, Shari Bowden, Robin Holcomb, and Kim Holly; (third row) Jane McCants, Judy Holly, and Betty Jo Vining Bowden. (Courtesy of the *Leader-Tribune*.)

Brownie Troop No. 246 is pictured here in 1972. In the photograph are, from left to right, (first row) Beth Greer Pearson, Virginia Nichols Culbreath, Wanda Hannon Barrett, Jessica Johnson, Denise Tripp, Hannah Moorman, and Melissa Cobb; (second row) Keith Rod, Angela Jones, Kimberly Bryan Ford, Beth Hodge Cameron, Cheryl Scott, Penny Campbell, and Tricia Eubanks Alford. (Courtesy of the *Leader-Tribune*.)

In this image are the charter members of the Fort Valley Kiwanis Club, as listed with this photograph in 1922. They are, from left to right, (first row) J.A. Beddingfield, Interlocking Rim Co. and fireman; John David Duke, farmer; A.C. Riley Sr., judge; L. Warwick, minister; Leighton Shepard, attorney; Ralph Newton, professor; Ed Murray, banker; R.D. Hale, Gallaher-Hall Grocery Co.; F.O. Miller, businessman; Moss Copeland, pharmacist; W. Brisendine, Coca-Cola bottler; and Dave Strother, Fort Valley Oil Company and Massee Lane Gardens; (second row) Harris Neil, mayor; A.M. Siefert, postmaster and Georgia Fruit Exchange; Glenmore Green, Green-Miller Co.; E.G. Clark; Dr. W.L. Nance, dentist; John Cook, Fruit Belt Telephone Co.; Russell Edwards, merchant; J.D. Fagan, farmer; N.W. Jordan Sr., city clerk; J.R. McDonald, Winona Hotel; Dr. Marcus Hickson, physician; J. Strickland, auto company; A.C. Riley Jr., Long Loans and lawyer; Fred Hume; B.T. Marshall, Marshall Grocery Co.; and Joel Mann Martin, editor of the *Leader-Tribune*. (Courtesy of W.L. Brown.)

Seen here is a pinewood derby at the Fort Valley United Methodist Fellowship Hall with Cub Scout Troop No. 59 around 1978. Participating in a pinewood derby has become a rite of passage for boys. A pinewood racing car program has been active since 1934. It was a good indoor Cub Scout project during the colder winter season. The Scout is given a block of pinewood to carve into a car, four plastic wheels, and four rails. The completed car must use all nine pieces, make a weight limit, and fit the track. (Courtesy of the *Leader-Tribune*.)

Stamps Baxter performs at a Blue Bird employee barbecue in June 1948. They were a professional gospel music group. Blue Bird employees were given the option of attending a 30-minute worship service and then taking a 30-minute lunch on Wednesdays or just taking a 30-minute lunch break. (Courtesy of Blue Bird Body Company.)

The Fort Valley Methodist Church Men's Bible Class was known as the "Railroad Men's Class" for its 23 members working for the railroads. On the day this photograph was taken—April 25, 1937—a total of 122 attended, making it one of the largest Bible classes in the state. Shown from left to right are (first row) J.B. Belcher, flagman; L.E. Houston, chief clerk; F.B. Little, class president; George B. Culpepper Jr., class teacher; R.L. Duke, operator; Lowell Parks, flagman; E.M. McAfee, conductor; Capt. Bob Flournoy, retired railroad worker; and W.R. Bittick, engineer; (second row) C.R. Hill Jr., flagman; C.H. Sammons, agent; L.M. Mills, supervisor; Bob Fagan, assistant rail welder; G.C. Visage, section foreman; J.M. Ross, section foreman; H.H. Howell, clerk-operator; and G.W. Spear, bridge foreman; (third row) Tom Bateman, clerk, Railway Express Agency; C.W. Walton, Railway Express agent; Opie Capps, track walker; Carlton Visage, track walker; Hugh Hill, Railway Express clerk; J.W. Davis, section foreman; and C.R. Hill, pumper.

All of the churches in Fort Valley, regardless of affiliation, sponsor a number of special projects to benefit the entire community. It takes the commitment and hard work of the congregations' members to make that possible. Pictured here in Shiloh Baptist Church, from left to right, are John Ezell, Bob Church, Rev. Morris Hillsman (Shiloh Baptist), H.E. Bryant, Rev. Charles Martin Jr. (Shiloh Baptist), Rev. Julius Simmons (Trinity Baptist), and Rev. James Webb (St. Peter's A.M.E.). (Courtesy of Wilmetta Langston.)

The Fort Valley Police Department is pictured in the 1960s. Officers are, from left to right, (first row) Boisey Barfield, Carl Ogletree, Virginia Clark, Chief Grady Cochran, J.T. Tucker, and R.L. Baggarly; (second row) David Humber, unidentified, W.M. Folsom, W.M. Worsham, and B.F. Hill; (third row) Odell Harp, unidentified, Jack Hodge, Robert Coberhouse, and Johnnie Becham. Cochran is credited with starting the first junior police program in the country and received an award signed by FBI director J. Edgar Hoover for his program. In 1996, Jerry Stripling Sr. became Fort Valley's first African American police chief.

The Fort Valley Fire Department in 1948–1949 is pictured in front of its old location downtown behind City TV. Firefighters are, from left to right, (first row) J.E. Jones, Harold Estes, Wilson Bryant, J.E. Brown, and Frank Wheeler; (second row) Gus Wouvis, T.A. Jones, Clinton Hutto, J.H. Hallman, Kelly Smith, N.W. Jordan, Robert Wells, T.M. Anthoine, C.E. Hutto, W.B. Hardeman, R.L. Baggarly, Olney Jones, and George Middlebrooks; W.E. Hannon is in the truck. (Courtesy of Todd Bryan.)

The members of the Fort Valley Fire Department in 1989 are shown in front of a fire truck. Several of these men were volunteers for both the Peach County Fire Department, formed in 1973, and the city. Pictured from left to right are (first row) Zeke Harvey, Phil Stephens, Todd Bryan, Joe Harvey, and Jimmy Hester; (second row) John Harmon, Ray Anthoine, Charles Smith, Karry Dailey, Jerry Bryan, and Charles Bryan; (third row) Willie Harvey, Maxie Gray, Jeff Doles, Alan Whittington, and Joe Martel. (Courtesy of Todd Bryan.)

During the devastating tornado of February 18, 1975, many of the Main Street businesses sustained considerable damages. The F3 tornado, with maximum winds of 158 to 206 miles per hour, entered the city at 4:10 p.m. from the west and left a path of destruction, ripping the fronts off nearly every building on both sides of Church and Main Streets. Shiloh Baptist Church on Griffin Line was destroyed. Two people were killed, 50 were injured, and damages were estimated at between $5 and $50 million. (Courtesy of the *Leader-Tribune*.)

This car belonged to a salesman calling on Jordan Electric. The salesman survived unscathed, but his car was a total loss. One month later, this same man had another car destroyed by a tornado in Atlanta. Once again, he was not hurt, but his car was totaled. From left to right are Larry Lee, Johnny Humble, Harry Sims, and Jimmy Guthrie. (Courtesy of the *Leader-Tribune*.)

In 1973, a record 16 inches of snow fell—the most snowfall to besiege the city. Pictured here is Anderson Avenue. The blizzard shut the state down for days. Power lines and trees fell under the weight of snow and ice. (Courtesy of the *Leader-Tribune.*)

The Pearson Packing Company on Vineville Street was fully engulfed in flames in 1976. According to the FVFD records, firefighters fought the blaze for 4 hours and 15 minutes, and it was a total loss. (Courtesy of Todd Bryan.)

On January 8, 1972, the fire at Lowe's Hardware Store was major and took more than five hours to extinguish. The two-story section used as a warehouse did not survive the fire. It had long ago been part of the New Dixie Hotel, which faced Railroad Street. (Courtesy of the *Leader-Tribune*.)

On the extremely cold morning of January 9, 1971, at about 6:00 a.m., the FVFD was dispatched to a fire just a block from the fire station at city hall. The fire started in Christopher's Furniture Store and quickly spread to Elrod's Five and Ten Store. Flames burst through Elrod's second floor and threatened Herbert Jewelers next door. It took more than 15 hours and two days of firefighting, but the two businesses could not be saved and were a total loss. Peggy Herbert (wearing the white hat) stands next to her father-in-law, Neal Herbert. Dennis Herbert took this photograph. (Courtesy of Dennis and Peggy Childree Herbert.)

Judge Millard C. Moseley, ordinary and county manager, proposed constructing an annex to be used as the Thomas Public Library when planning the 1936 Peach County Courthouse. The library was separated by a firewall and had a separate entrance on Central Avenue. On December 5, 1969, a fire gutted the library, burning 15,000 books, and anything that remained was water damaged. The December 11, 1969, edition of the *Leader-Tribune* reported the fire was suspicious and ruled as arson.

Fort Valley has survived many fires and other catastrophes by working together and helping those in need. It was no different when it came to replacing the Thomas Public Library after the courthouse fire. Pictured are some of those generous men and women who pulled together for the benefit of all.

Fort Valley celebrated its sesquicentennial in March 2006 and looks forward to the next 150 years. (Courtesy of Dennis and Peggy Childree Herbert.)

Part of the pageantry and tradition of the modern Georgia Peach Festival is the crowning of the Peach Queens. Seen here are the 2012 Miss Georgia Peach Queens in front of bins of peaches donated by Pearson Farms and Lane Southern Orchards. From left to right are Tiny Miss Georgia Peach Brynn Owens, Junior Miss Georgia Peach Kaitlyn Bustamante, Little Miss Georgia Peach Lauren Roberts, Miss Georgia Peach Anna Treadway, Teen Miss Georgia Peach Cassidy Starling, and Devon Davis eating a peach. (Courtesy of Steve Nowicki.)

Bibliography

Bellamy, Donnie D. *From Slavery to Freedom: A Pictorial History of Shiloh Missionary Baptist Church since 1863*. Virginia Beach: Donning, 1998.

———. *Light in the Valley*. Virginia Beach: Donning, 1996.

Brown, Thelma R. and Dollie D. Horton, eds. *Fort Valley, A Story Untold*. Fort Valley: Thelma R. Brown, 2000.

Governor Treutlen Chapter, Daughters of the American Revolution. *History of Peach County, Georgia*. Atlanta: Cherokee, 1972.

Hay, Guelda L., Millie C. Stewart, and Davine V. Campbell. *Oaklawn Cemetery, Fort Valley, Georgia, 1850–1993*. Warner Robins: Central Georgia Genealogical Society, 1995.

Leslie, Sue. "The Peach Blossom Festivals." Local History Collection, Peach Public Libraries.

Little, Capt. Autry, and Capt. Otis Daniels. *Call to Duty, Fort Valley Fire Department*. L. Lavery & Company, 1996.

Palmer, Bernard. *Wings of Blue Bird*. Columbia, SC: R.L. Bryan, 1977.

Powell, Billy. *Echoes from the Valley*. Macon: Indigo Custom Publishing, 2006.

Windham, Marilyn N. *Peach County: The World's Peach Paradise*. Charleston, SC: Arcadia Publishing, 1997.

Word, John, Willis James, and Lewis Jones, contributors. *Fort Valley Blues, Library of Congress Field Recordings from Georgia, Vol. II*. Matchbox-Flyright Records, 1973.

www.fortvalleymainstreet.org

www.fortvalleyusa.com

www.fvsu.edu

www.gapeachfestival.com

www.jollynut.com

www.kommish.net

www.lanepacking.com

www.peach.public.lib.ga.us

www.pearsonfarm.com

www.pineola.com

www.sos.ga.gov/archives/

Consistent with our mission to preserve history on a local level, this book was printed in South Carolina on American-made paper and manufactured entirely in the United States. Products carrying the accredited Forest Stewardship Council (FSC) label are printed on 100 percent FSC-certified paper.